Managing Editor
Mara Ellen Guckian

Illustrator
Kelly McMahon

Editor in Chief
Ina Massler Levin, M.A.

Creative Director
Karen J. Goldfluss, M.S. Ed.

Cover Artist
Barb Lorseyedi

Art Coordinator
Renée Mc Elwee

Imaging
Craig Gunnell

Publisher
Mary D. Smith, M.S. Ed.

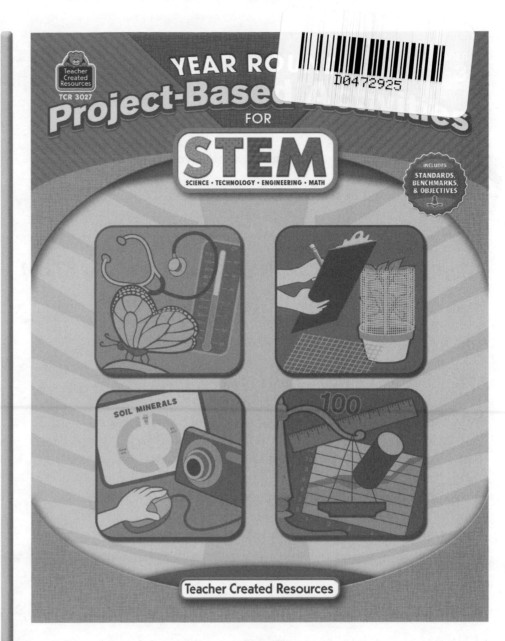

Author

Steve Butz, M. A. T.

The classroom teacher may reproduce the materials in this book and/or CD for use in a single classroom only. The reproduction of any part of this book and/or CD for other classrooms or for an entire school or school system is strictly prohibited. No part of this publication may be transmitted or recorded in any form without written permission from the publisher with the exception of electronic material, which may be stored on the purchaser's computer only.

Teacher Created Resources
6421 Industry Way
Westminster, CA 92683
www.teachercreated.com
ISBN 978 1-4206-3027-5

© 2013 Teacher Created Resources
Made in U.S.A.

Table of Contents

Project-Based Units for STEM

Introduction

The increased use of Science, Technology, Engineering, and Math (STEM) in the elementary classroom is an important step toward the goal of preparing our students for success in the 21st century. *Year Round Project-Based Activities for STEM* is a hands-on activity book that provides STEM-based projects for science, technology, engineering, and math. The elementary classroom is the perfect place to introduce project-based learning because it incorporates both academic and technological skills that draw on students with different skill sets, backgrounds, and ideas.

This book provides many opportunities to learn-while-doing. It also encourages students to think critically, and be proactive in their own education. We have seen that project-based learning tends to be a deeper learning experience, which is often more relevant to students and thus is more easily retained. Project-based learning and STEM dovetail perfectly, guaranteeing that 21st century skills such as collaboration, communication, critical thinking, problem solving, and digital literacy are incorporated into the curriculum while supporting students' academic and socio-emotional growth. Further, project-based learning allows teachers to almost immediately conduct authentic assessments to gauge what students comprehend, helping them to adapt the curriculum accordingly. Most of all, project-based learning is fun!

Standards, Benchmarks, and Learning Objectives

Each lesson in *Year Round Project-Based Activities for STEM* meets one or more of the following standards for Science Technology, and Mathematics, which are used with permission from McREL (Copyright 2011 McREL, Mid-continent Research for Education and Learning. Telephone 303-337-0990. (*www.mcrel. org.*). To align McREL Standards to the Common Core Standards go to *www.mcrel.org*. Additionally, age-appropriate learning objectives have been suggested for Engineering.

Science

Understands atmospheric processes and the water cycle
➡ Knows that water can be a liquid or a solid and can be made to change from one form to the other, but the amount of water stays the same
➡ Knows that water exists in the air in different forms (e.g., in clouds and fog as tiny droplets; in rain, snow, and hail) and changes from one form to another through various processes (e.g., freezing, condensation, precipitation, evaporation)

Understands Earth's composition and structure
➡ Knows that Earth materials consist of solid rocks, soils, liquid water, and the gases of the atmosphere
➡ Knows that rocks come in many different shapes and sizes (e.g., boulders, pebbles, sand)
➡ Knows how features on the Earth's surface are constantly changed by a combination of slow and rapid processes (e.g., weathering, erosion, transport, and deposition of sediment caused by waves, wind, water, and ice; landslides, volcanic eruptions, earthquakes, drought)
➡ Knows that smaller rocks come from the weathering and breakage of larger rocks and bedrock
➡ Knows the composition and properties of soils (e.g., components of soil such as weathered rock, living organisms, products of plants and animals; properties of soil such as color, texture, capacity to retain water, ability to support plant growth)

Understands the structure and function of cells and organisms
➡ Knows the basic needs of plants and animals (e.g., air, water, nutrients, light or food, shelter)
➡ Knows that plants and animals progress through life cycles of birth, growth and development, reproduction, and death; the details of these life cycles are different for different organisms
➡ Knows that living organisms have distinct structures and body systems that serve specific functions in growth, survival, and reproductions (e.g., various body structures for walking, flying or swimming)

Understands the relationships among organisms and their physical environment
➡ Knows that plants and animals need certain resources for energy and growth
(e.g., food, water, light, air)
➡ Knows that changes in the environment can have different effects on different organisms
(e.g., some organisms move in, others move out; some organisms survive and reproduce, others die)

Understands the structure and properties of matter
➡ Knows that different objects are made up of many different types of materials (e.g., cloth, paper, wood, metal) and have many different observable properties (e.g., color, size, shape, weight)
➡ Knows that things can be done to materials to change some of their properties (e.g., heating, freezing, mixing, cutting, dissolving, bending), but not all materials respond the same way to what is done to them
➡ Knows that matter has different states (i.e., liquid, solid, gas) and that each state has distinct physical properties; some common materials such as water can be changed from one state to another by heating or cooling

Standards, Benchmarks, and Learning Objectives (*cont.*)

Science (*cont.*)

Understands the nature of scientific knowledge

➡ Knows that scientific investigations generally work the same way in different places and normally produce results that can be duplicated

➡ Knows that although the same scientific investigation may give slightly different results when it is carried out by different persons, or at different times or places, the general evidence collected from the investigation should be replicated by others

➡ Knows that good scientific explanations are based on evidence (observations) and scientific knowledge

➡ Knows that scientists make the results of their investigations public; they describe the investigations in ways that enable others to repeat the investigations

➡ Knows that scientists review and ask questions about the results of other scientists' work

Understands the nature of scientific inquiry

➡ Knows that learning can come from careful observations and simple experiments

➡ Knows that tools (e.g., thermometers, magnifiers, rulers, balances) can be used to gather information

➡ Knows that scientific investigations involve asking and answering a question and comparing the answer to what scientists already know about the world

➡ Plans and conducts simple investigations (e.g., formulates a testable question, makes systematic observations, develops logical conclusions)

➡ Uses appropriate tools and simple equipment (e.g., thermometers, magnifiers, microscopes, calculators, graduated cylinders) to gather scientific data and extend the senses

Understands the scientific enterprise

➡ Knows that in science it is helpful to work with a team and share findings with others

➡ Knows that scientists and engineers often work in teams to accomplish a task

Technology

Understands the characteristics and uses of computer hardware and operating systems

➡ Knows basic computer hardware (e.g., keyboard and mouse, printer and monitor, optical storage device [such as CD-ROM], case for the CPU [central processing unit])

➡ Knows the basic functions of hardware (e.g., keyboard and mouse provide input; printer and monitor provide output; optical discs such as CD-ROMs provide storage; the CPU processes information)

Understands the characteristics and uses of computer software programs

➡ Knows basic features of computer software (e.g., file, open, save, help, preview)

➡ Uses a word processor to edit, copy, move, save, and print text with some formatting (e.g., centering lines, using tabs, forming paragraphs)

Understands the relationships among science, technology, society, and the individual

➡ Knows ways that technology is used at home and at school (e.g., computers, cell phones, DVD players)

➡ Knows that new inventions often lead to other new inventions and ways of doing things

Understands the nature of technological design

➡ Knows that tools have specific functions, such as to observe, measure, make things, and do things better or more easily; selecting the right tool makes the task easier

➡ Knows that group collaboration is useful as the combination of multiple creative minds can yield more possible design solutions

Engineering Learning Objectives

Uses engineering design to pose questions, seek answers, and develop solutions

- ➡ Identifies simple problems and solutions
- ➡ Understands troubleshooting procedures
- ➡ Proposes alternative solutions for procedures
- ➡ Uses a variety of verbal and graphic techniques to present conclusions
- ➡ Devises ways to determine the volume of a solid object

Mathematics

Uses a variety of strategies in the problem-solving process

- ➡ Uses discussions with teachers and other students to understand problems
- ➡ Makes organized lists or tables of information necessary for solving a problem

Understands and applies basic and advanced properties of the concepts of numbers

- ➡ Counts whole numbers (i.e., both cardinal and ordinal numbers)
- ➡ Understands symbolic, concrete, and pictorial representations of numbers (e.g., written numerals, objects in sets, number lines)
- ➡ Uses models (e.g., number lines, two-dimensional and three-dimensional regions) to identify, order, and compare numbers

Uses basic and advanced procedures while performing the processes of computation

Understands and applies basic and advanced properties of the concepts of measurement

- ➡ Understands the basic measures length, width, height, weight, and temperature
- ➡ Selects and uses appropriate tools for given measurement situations (e.g., rulers for length, measuring cups for capacity, protractors for angles)

Understands and applies basic and advanced concepts of statistics and data analysis

- ➡ Collects and represents information about objects or events in simple graphs
- ➡ Understands that one can find out about a group of things by studying just a few of them
- ➡ Understands that data represent specific pieces of information about real-world objects or activities
- ➡ Reads and interprets data in charts, tables, and plots (e.g., stem-and-leaf, box-and-whiskers, scatter)
- ➡ Reads and interprets simple bar graphs, pie charts, and line graphs
- ➡ Understands that data come in many different forms and that collecting, organizing, and displaying data can be done in many ways

Understands and applies basic and advanced concepts of probability

- ➡ Understands that some events can be predicted fairly well but others cannot because we do not always know everything that may affect an event
- ➡ Recognizes events that are sure to happen, events that are sure not to happen, and events that may or may not happen (e.g., in terms of "certain," "uncertain," "likely," "unlikely")

Understands the general nature and uses of mathematics

- ➡ Understands that numbers and the operations performed on them can be used to describe things in the real world and predict what might occur

Why Project-Based Learning?

Year Round Project-Based Activities for STEM presents 12 activities that can be easily implemented within 2nd and 3rd grade classrooms. The activities are divided to cover both the physical and biological sciences. Each activity in the book provides clear learning standards and objectives in science, math, engineering, and technology. The activities are designed for use in the classroom, with materials that can be easily obtained.

Each activity begins with background information, a materials list, and a vocabulary list (with definitions pertinent to the specific activity) that will help prepare your students for the content of the lesson. Clear, step-by-step procedures are provided that can be used by both the students and the teacher. The activities in the book are centered around hands-on scientific investigations, which allow students to use the scientific method to answer questions about the living and non-living world. The activities also involve the applied use of mathematics, to help students solve problems.

The use of brainstorming sessions during the activities gives teachers and students the opportunity to incorporate more engineering (creative thinking) into the science curriculum. By posing "what if we tried…" and "how might we improve…" -type questions, students are encouraged to think more deeply about the activities and to try different approaches. Students are also encouraged to design and build to turn their ideas into reality. It is not always about the right answer, but about the exploration.

All activities within the book culminate with the use of computer technology. Students take the data they have gathered from their scientific investigations and use common word-processing, drawing, or spreadsheet software to analyze and present it. The computer technology portion of each activity also comes with clear, step-by-step procedures, including screenshots, making it very easy for students to work individually. The computer portion of each activity is designed to be done in a computer lab setting but can be done in the classroom using fewer computers and collaborating in small groups. The goal is to allow each student to have the opportunity to apply the use of technology to the project. Useful tables, diagrams, and reproducibles are also provided where needed within each activity.

Teachers will find this book filled with many useful ways to engage students in learning about science, while also incorporating technology, engineering, and math into their 2nd or 3rd grade curricula.

Vocabulary for the 21st Century

apply	determine	innovate
arrange	develop	inquire
assess	discover	invent
brainstorm	discuss	investigate
build	dramatize	list
challenge	evaluate	listen
chart	figure out	model
collaborate	graph	organize
communicate	gather	plan
complete	imagine	practice
consider	implement	problem-solve
construct	improve	relate (relevant)
create	incorporate	research
critique	improvise	review
design	initiate	support

Weathering Rocks

Stem Project Overview

Students will collaborate to:

➡ Observe how the weathering of rocks can occur by the process of abrasion in water. (***Science/Math***)

➡ Enter the Weathering Rocks data collected during an experiment into a spreadsheet. (***Science/Technology/Math***)

➡ Display the data in the form of a line chart. (***Technology/Engineering/Math***)

➡ Evaluate their findings. (***Science/Math***)

➡ Brainstorm to improve the experimentation process. (***Science/Engineering***)

Science

Students will understand the Earth's composition and structure, including:

- Knowing how features on the Earth's surface are constantly changed by a combination of slow and rapid processes, including weathering erosion and transport

- Knowing that smaller rocks come from the weathering and breakage of larger rocks

Math

Students will use mathematical analysis to pose questions, seek answers, and develop solutions, including:

- Selecting the appropriate operation to solve mathematical problems

- Applying mathematical skills to describe the natural world

- Using appropriate scientific tools to solve problems about the natural world

Engineering

Students will use engineering design to pose questions, seek answers, and develop solutions, including:

- Proposing alternative solutions for procedures

- Using a variety of verbal and graphic techniques to present conclusions

- Identifying simple problems and solutions

- Understanding troubleshooting procedures

Technology

Students will know the characteristics, uses, and basic features of computer software programs, including:

- Knowing the common features and uses of spreadsheets

- Using spreadsheet software to update, add and delete data, and to produce charts

Weathering Rocks *(cont.)*

Materials

- marble chips (per group) can be purchased at home-and-garden or hardware stores
- paper towels
- scale or balance (per group)
- sink or large bucket
- small, plastic 8 oz. jar with lid (per group)
- stopwatch (per group)
- strainer or sieve (per group)

Vocabulary

abrade—to wear away by scraping or erosion

mass—the amount of matter an object contains

gram—a metric unit for mass

weathering—the breakdown of rocks into smaller pieces

Background

Before beginning this experiment, soak the marble chips (rocks) in water. Since this activity involves the use of water to *abrade* the marble chips, it is important to start with wet ones. This is because water has *mass* and can affect the results when the marble chips are weighed.

Science Experiment Procedure

1. Use a balance or scale to weigh out approximately 20 grams of damp marble chips.
2. Lay out a paper towel and carefully pour out the marble chips onto it. Use the paper towel to dry off the marble chips as much as possible.
3. Weigh the marble chips once again and record the start mass at time zero in your Weathering Rocks data table like the one shown below. Also record the appearance of the water in your data table. See page 12 for data table templates.

Weathering Rocks		
Time (minutes)	**Mass (grams)**	**Observations**
0	21 grams	Water is clear.
3		
6		
9		
12		
15		
Total Mass Lost		

Weathering Rocks *(cont.)*

Science Experiment Procedure *(cont.)*

4. Pour the marble chips into a plastic jar. Add just enough water to cover them.

5. Screw the lid onto the jar tightly.

6. Begin to shake the jar vigorously and start the stopwatch. Shake the marble chips for 3 minutes.

7. After 3 minutes, stop shaking the jar. Observe the appearance of the water and record it in your data table.

8. Open the jar. Pour the marble chips into the strainer over the sink or a bucket.

9. Lay out a dry paper towel and carefully pour the wet marble chips onto it. Use the paper towel to dry off the marble chips.

10. Weigh the marble chips and record their mass under Mass in the Time column for 3 minutes, in your data table.

11. Pour the marble chips back into the jar and add just enough water to cover them.

12. Place the lid on the jar tightly and begin to shake them again for another 3 minutes.

13. After 3 minutes, repeat steps 9, 10, and 11. Continue the same process every 3 minutes until you have shaken the marble chips for a total of 15 minutes.

14. Record the Mass at each 3-minute interval.

15. Now that your experiment is complete, you will determine the total mass of rock that was lost by the weathering process. To do this, subtract the mass of the marble chips at 15 minutes, from the mass of the marble chips at the start of the experiment. Then record the Total Mass Lost in your data table.

Brainstorming

Once the class has completed the activity, ask students if they can think of any ways that the experiment could be improved. For example, is there a way to make the process of shaking the marble chips more efficient? What about a different way to strain or dry the marble chips? Can students devise a different system for weighing the chips?

Weathering Rocks *(cont.)*

Science Experiment Procedure *(cont.)*

Weathering Rocks Data Table Templates

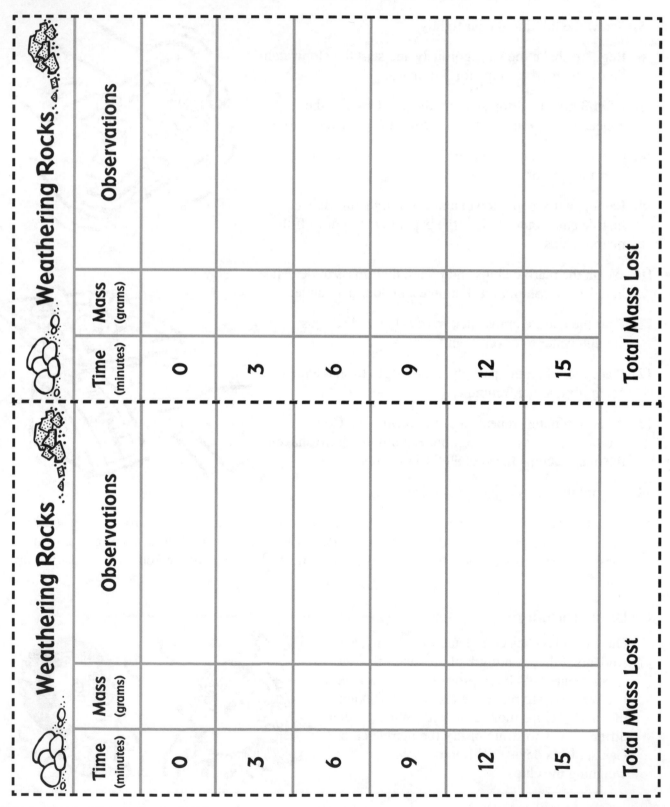

Weathering Rocks *(cont.)*

Technology Learning Objectives

At the end of this lesson, students will:

1. Know the various terms associated with spreadsheets including, rows, columns, and cells.

2. Enter data into a spreadsheet.

3. Adjust the width of a selected column.

4. Change the alignment of data within a cell.

5. Change the style of data within a cell.

6. Create and format a line chart from data entered within a spreadsheet.

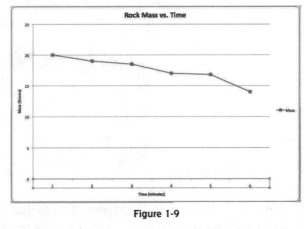

Figure 1-9

Teacher Note

The technology portion of this activity is written for MS Excel 2010 but can be completed using most spreadsheet and word processing software versions like Open Office, Google Docs, and iWorks with minimal modification.

Technology Procedure

1. Open a new spreadsheet document. Spreadsheets are made up of *columns* that are identified by letters (A, B, C, etc.) and *rows* that are identified by numbers (1, 2, 3, etc.).

2. The location within a spreadsheet where a column meets a row is called a *cell*. It is identified by both a letter and number (Figure 1-1).

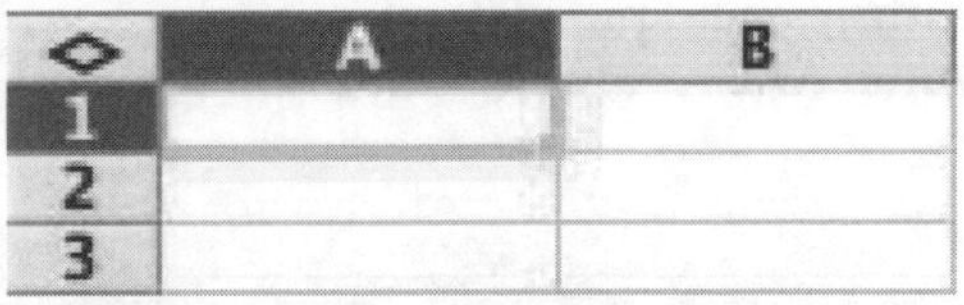

Figure 1-1

3. Click into cell **A1** and type in the following label, "Time (minutes)." Hit the **Tab** key on your keyboard to bring you over to cell **B1** and type in the label "Mass (grams)."

4. Next, click and drag over the two column labels. Use the **Bold** button on your toolbar to make your column titles bold (Figure 1-2).

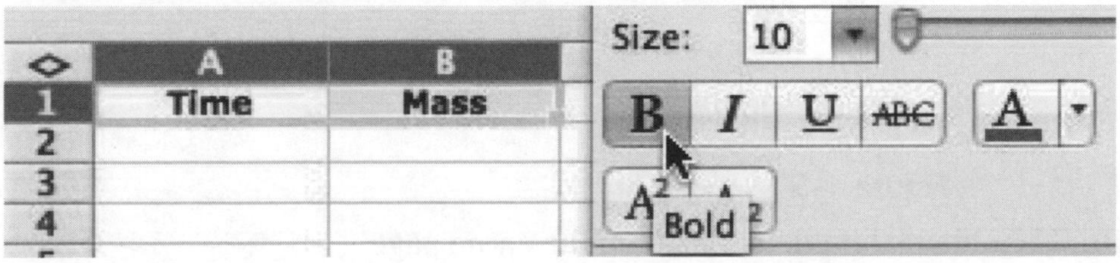

Figure 1-2

5. Now fill in the data into your spreadsheet.

Weathering Rocks *(cont.)*

Technology Procedure *(cont.)*

6. Next, you will center your data in your cells. To do this, click and drag over all of the data in your spreadsheet to highlight it. Then use the **Align Center** button on your toolbar (Figure 1-3).

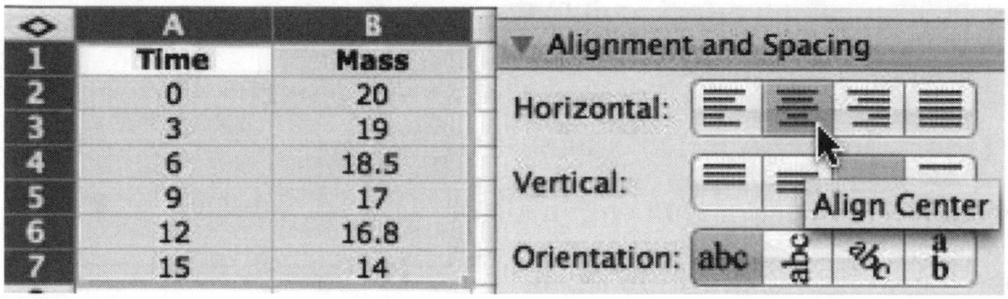

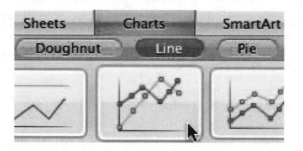

Figure 1-3

7. Now you are going to use your data to create a chart. First, highlight all of your data in both columns, including the labels. Choose the **Insert** menu, choose **Chart**, and click on **Line Chart or Line** (Figure 1-4).

Figure 1-4

8. Your chart should now appear within your spreadsheet.
9. Go to the **Chart** menu, select **Move Chart**, choose **New Sheet,** and click **OK**. (Figure 1-5).

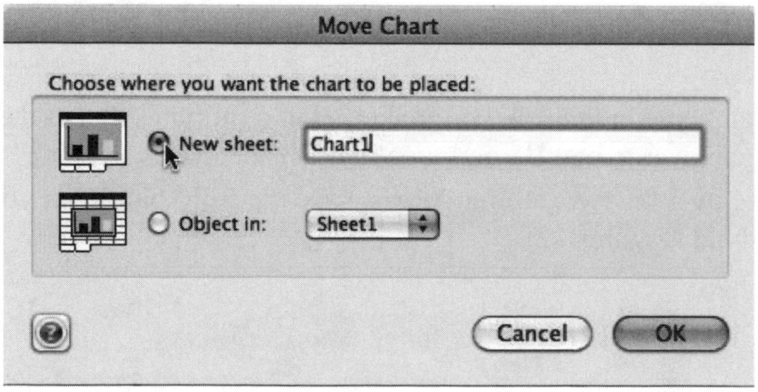

Figure 1-5

10. Your chart should now take up the entire page.

Weathering Rocks *(cont.)*

Technology Procedure *(cont.)*

11. Right click (Control-click on a Mac) on the blue line for **Time** and select **Delete** from the dropdown window. This will remove the time data from your spreadsheet (Figure 1-6).

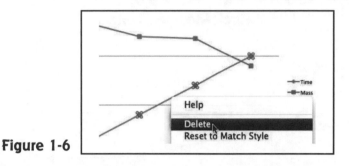

Figure 1-6

12. Next, under chart options in the **Chart Titles** box, type in: "Rock Mass vs. Time" (Figure 1-7).

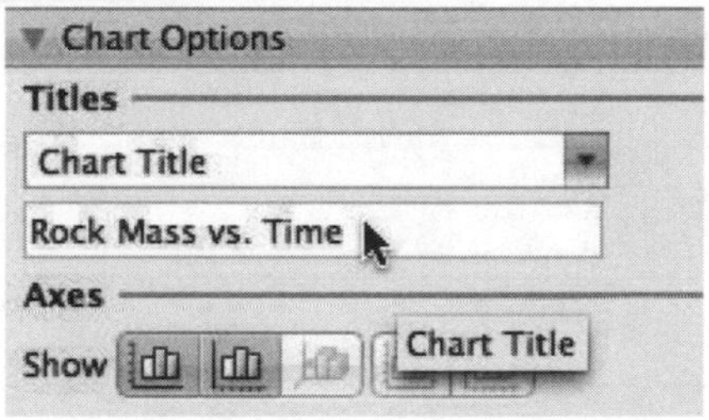

Figure 1-7

13. Under **Chart Options**, click on the **Chart Title** dropdown menu and select **Horizontal Category Axis**. Type in the following label for the horizontal axis: "Time (Minutes)" (Figure 1-8).

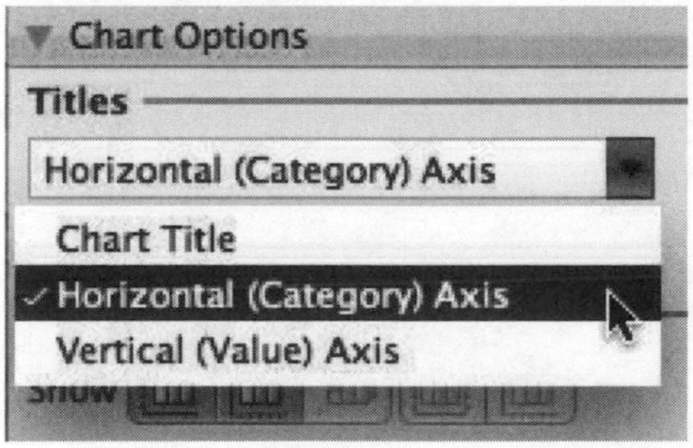

Figure 1-8

14. Next select the **Vertical Category Axis** from the **Titles** dropdown menu and type in: "Mass (Grams)."

Weathering Rocks *(cont.)*

Technology Procedure *(cont.)*

15. Save and **Print** the *Rock Mass vs. Time* chart. It should look similar to the one in Figure 1–9.

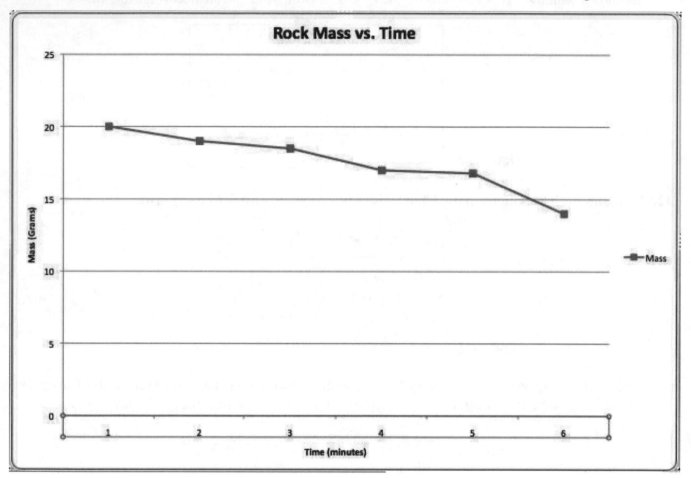

Figure 1-9

Pulse Rate

STEM Project Overview

Students will collaborate to:

➡ Observe how a person's pulse rate is affected by physical activity. *(Science/Math)*

➡ Enter the Pulse Rate data collected during an experiment into a spreadsheet. *(Science/Technology/Math)*

➡ Display their data in the form of a bar graph. *(Technology/Engineering/Math)*

➡ Evaluate their findings. *(Science/Math)*

➡ Brainstorm to improve the experimentation process. *(Science/Engineering)*

Science

Students will understand the structure and function of cells and organisms, including:

- Knowing that living organisms have distinct structures and body systems that serve specific functions

- Using appropriate tools and simple equipment to gather scientific data and extend the senses

- Knowing that learning can come from careful observations and simple experiments

Math

Students will use mathematical analysis to pose questions, seek answers, and develop solutions, including:

- Selecting the appropriate operation to solve mathematical problems

- Applying mathematical skills to describe the natural world

- Using appropriate scientific tools to solve problems about the natural world

- Using representations such as pictures, charts, and tables from the investigation of mathematical ideas

Engineering

Students will use engineering design to pose questions, seek answers, and develop solutions, including:

- Identifying simple problems and solutions

- Using a variety of verbal and graphic techniques to present conclusions

- Understanding troubleshooting procedures

Technology

Students will know the characteristics, uses, and basic features of computer software programs, including:

- Knowing the common features and uses of spreadsheets

- Using spreadsheet software to update, add and delete data, and produce charts

Pulse Rate (cont.)

Materials

- clipboard (per group)
- stopwatch (per group)

Vocabulary

artery—tubes within the body that circulate blood from the heart
blood—the red liquid within the body that circulates oxygen
heart—the muscular organ that pumps blood through the body
pulse—the rhythmic throbbing of arteries within the wrist or neck

Background

Before beginning this experiment, have the students practice finding their pulse rate. The pulse can be felt by using the middle and index fingers gently applying pressure on the wrist or neck. **The pulse rate is calculated by counting the number of throbs within the artery over the course of a minute.** Also, discuss how the pulse rate is used to measure the beating of the heart and describe how the heart is responsible for a person's pulse rate.

Science Experiment Procedure

1. Make a Pulse Rate data table similar to the one in Table 2-1. You can also make copies of the data table template shown on page 19.

Pulse Rate	
Activity	**Beats Per Minute**
sitting in a chair	
after walking	
after 25 jumping jacks	

Table 2-1

2. Have a seat at the desk and reset the stopwatch to zero.
3. Find the pulse on the wrist (or neck) and practice counting the beats. When you are ready, start the stopwatch and count the number of beats for one minute.
4. After the minute is up, record the number of beats as the pulse rate. Then write the pulse rate data in the data table.
5. Reset the stopwatch, get up from the chair, walk over to the other end of the classroom, and then return to the desk.
6. Start the stopwatch and count the beats of the pulse for one minute. Record the pulse rate data in the data table.
7. Now, reset the stopwatch and do 25 jumping jacks.
8. After the jumping jacks, start the stopwatch and count the beats of the pulse for one minute. Record the pulse rate data in the data table.

Brainstorming

Once the class has completed the activity, ask students if they can think of any ways that the experiment could be improved. For example, how could a group of two or three students work together to determine their pulse rates?

Pulse Rate *(cont.)*

Science Experiment Procedure *(cont.)*

***Pulse Rate* Data Table Templates**

Pulse Rate	
Activity	**Beats Per Minute**
while sitting in a chair	
after walking	
after 25 jumping jacks	

Pulse Rate	
Activity	**Beats Per Minute**
while sitting in a chair	
after walking	
after 25 jumping jacks	

Pulse Rate (cont.)

Technology Learning Objectives

At the end of this lesson, students will:

1. Know the various terms associated with spreadsheets including rows, columns, and cells.
2. Enter data into a spreadsheet.
3. Adjust the width of a selected column.
4. Change the alignment of data within a cell.
5. Change the style of data within a cell.
6. Create and format a bar graph from data entered within a spreadsheet.

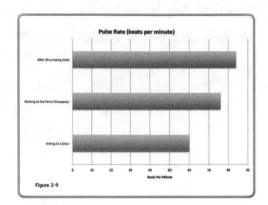

Figure 2-9

Teacher Note

The technology portion of this activity is written for MS Excel 2010 but can be completed using most spreadsheet and word processing software versions like Open Office, Google Docs, and iWorks with minimal modification.

Technology Procedure

1. Open a new spreadsheet document. Spreadsheets are made up of *columns* that are identified by letters (A, B, C, etc.) and *rows* that are identified by numbers (1, 2, 3, etc.).
2. The location within a spreadsheet where a column meets a row is called a *cell*. It is identified by both a letter and number (Figure 2-1).

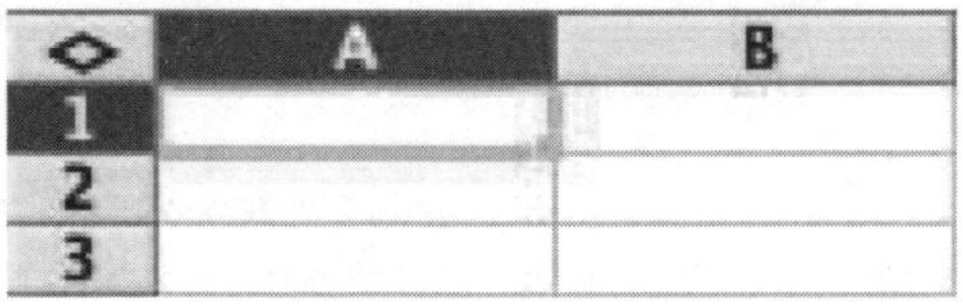

Figure 2-1

3. Click into cell **A1** and type in the following label: "Activity." Hit the **Tab** key on the keyboard to bring you over to cell **B1** and type in the label: "Pulse Rate (beats per minute)."
4. Next, click and drag over the two column labels and use the **Bold** button on the toolbar to make the column titles bold (Figure 2-2).

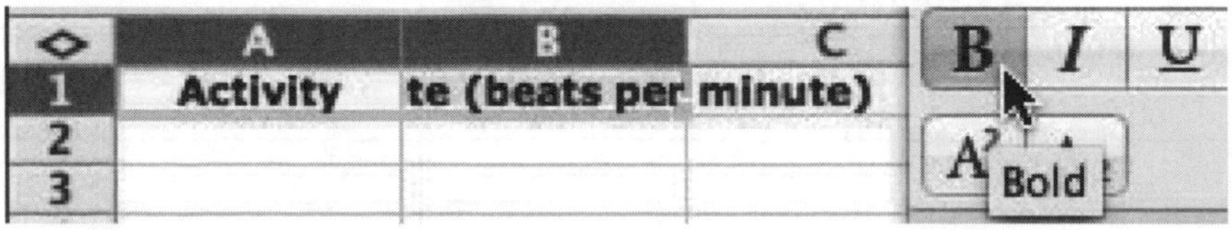

Figure 2-2

Pulse Rate *(cont.)*

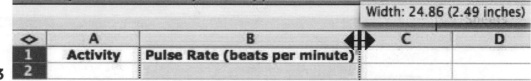

Technology Procedure *(cont.)*

5. Widen column B so that its label fits within the cell. To do this, use the mouse to move the cursor over the line between columns B and C at the top of the spreadsheet. Then click and drag it to the right until the column is wide enough for the label to fit (Figure 2-3).

Figure 2-3

	A	B	C	D
		Width: 24.86 (2.49 inches)		
1	Activity	Pulse Rate (beats per minute)		
2				

6. Next, enter the data you gathered on the three different pulse rates into the spreadsheet (Figure 2-4).

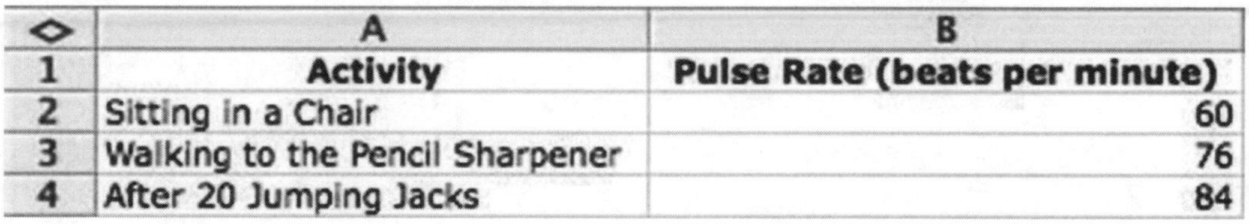

Figure 2-4

	A	B
1	Activity	Pulse Rate (beats per minute)
2	Sitting in a Chair	60
3	Walking to the Pencil Sharpener	76
4	After 20 Jumping Jacks	84

7. Center the data in the cells. To do this, click and drag over all of the data in the spreadsheet to highlight it. Then use the **Align Center** button on the toolbar (Figure 2-5).

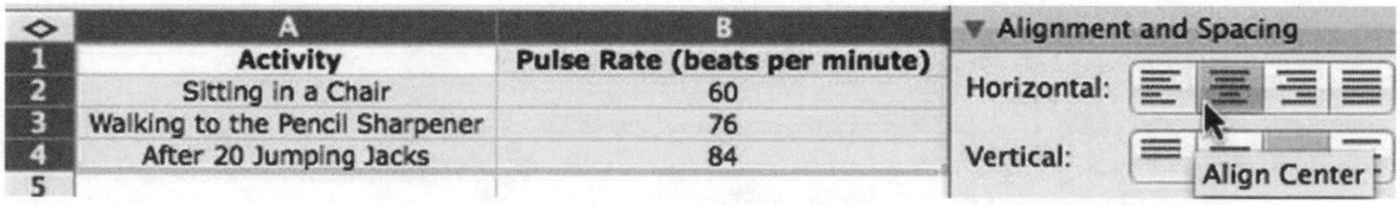

Figure 2-5

	A	B
1	Activity	Pulse Rate (beats per minute)
2	Sitting in a Chair	60
3	Walking to the Pencil Sharpener	76
4	After 20 Jumping Jacks	84
5		

▼ Alignment and Spacing

Horizontal:

Vertical:
Align Center

8. Now use the data to create a chart. Keep the data highlighted in both columns, including the labels. Choose the **Insert** menu, select **Chart**, and click on **Bar** (Figure 2-6).

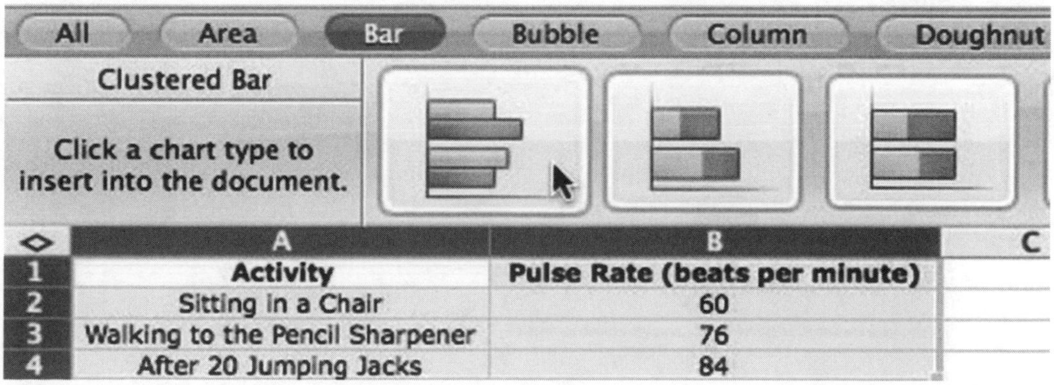

Figure 2-6

| All | Area | Bar | Bubble | Column | Doughnut |

Clustered Bar

Click a chart type to insert into the document.

	A	B	C
1	Activity	Pulse Rate (beats per minute)	
2	Sitting in a Chair	60	
3	Walking to the Pencil Sharpener	76	
4	After 20 Jumping Jacks	84	

Pulse Rate *(cont.)*

Technology Procedure *(cont.)*

9. Your bar chart should now be shown within the spreadsheet. Next, you are going to make it fit on one page. To do this, select the **Chart** menu and choose **Move Chart**.   Now select **New Sheet** and click **OK** (Figure 2-7).

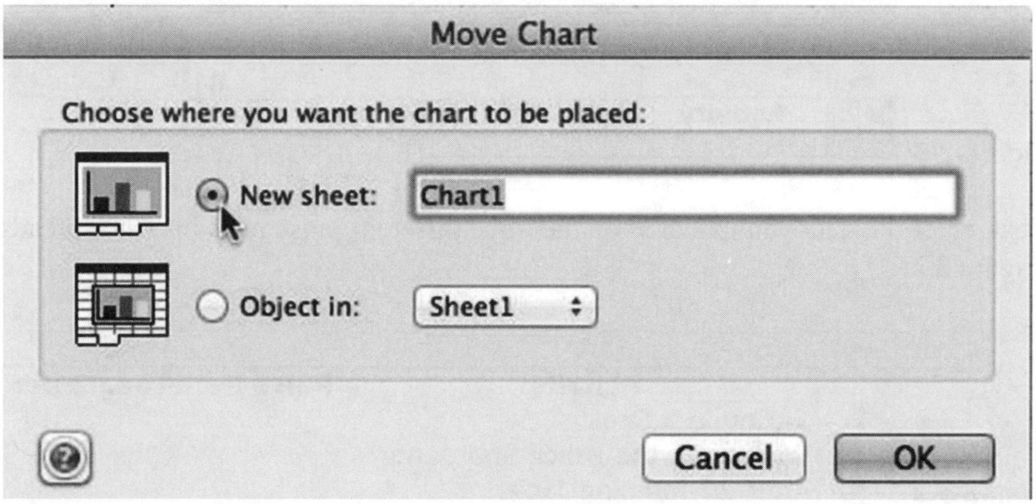

Figure 2-7

10. Finally, you will add labels to the chart. Select **Chart Options, Horizontal (Value) Axis** and type in the label: "Pulse Rate: Beats Per Minute" (Figure 2-8).

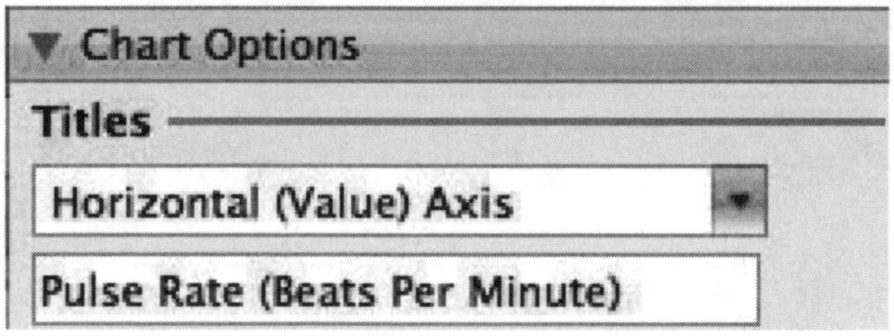

Figure 2-8

Pulse Rate *(cont.)*

Technology Procedure *(cont.)*

11. Now under **Legend**, choose **None** to remove the legend.

12. Your chart is now complete. **Save** and **Print**. It should look similar to the one in Figure 2-9.

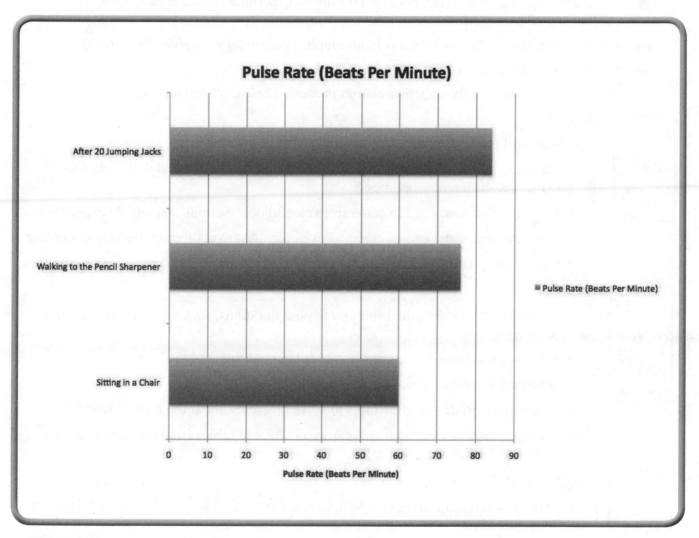

Figure 2-9

Phases of Water

STEM Project Overview

Students will collaborate to:

➡ Observe how the three states of matter have different temperatures. *(Science/Math)*

➡ Enter the Phases of Water data collected during an experiment into a spreadsheet. *(Science/Technology/Math)*

➡ Display their data in the form of a column graph. *(Technology/Engineering/Math)*

➡ Evaluate their findings. *(Science/Math)*

➡ Brainstorm to improve the experimentation process. *(Science/Engineering)*

Science

Students will understand the structure and properties of matter, including:

- Knowing that matter has different states (solid, liquid, gas) and that each state of matter has different properties

- Knowing that learning can come from careful observations and simple experiments

- Knowing that water can be changed from one state to another by heating or cooling

- Using appropriate tools and simple equipment to gather scientific data and extend the senses

Math

Students will use mathematical analysis to pose questions, seek answers, and develop solutions, including:

- Selecting the appropriate operation to solve mathematical problems

- Applying mathematical skills to describe the natural world

- Using appropriate scientific tools to solve problems about the natural world

- Using representations such as pictures, charts, and tables from the investigation of mathematical ideas

Engineering

Students will use engineering design to pose questions, seek answers, and develop solutions, including:

- Proposing alternative solutions for procedures

- Using a variety of verbal and graphic techniques to present conclusions

- Identifying simple problems and solutions

- Understanding troubleshooting procedures

Technology

Students will know the characteristics, uses, and basic features of computer software programs, including:

- Knowing the common features and uses of spreadsheets

- Using spreadsheet software to update, add and delete data, and to produce charts

Phases of Water *(cont.)*

Materials

- Celsius thermometer (per group)
- Fahrenheit thermometer (per group)
- hot plate
- oven mitt
- ice cube (per group)
- pot or beaker filled with boiling water (enough for teacher demonstration)
- sample of room-temperature water (approx. 300 mL per group)
- stopwatch (per group)

Vocabulary

boiling point—the temperature at which liquid water turns into a gas (water vapor)

Celsius—a scale of temperature on which water freezes at 0° and boils at 100°
      C = Celsius

Fahrenheit—a scale of temperature on which water freezes at 32° and boils at 212°
      F = Fahrenheit

freezing point—the temperature at which liquid water turns into a solid (ice)

ice—the solid form of water

water vapor—the gaseous form of water

Background

Demonstrate to the students what happens to the temperature of the water within the beaker or pot when you apply heat to it in order to make it boil. **Go over the safety procedures about how you will help each student to take the temperature of the boiling water.**

Discuss the two different types of temperature scales, Celsius and Fahrenheit, and demonstrate how to correctly use a thermometer by using the bulb at the bottom.

Before beginning the experiment, make sure you have enough samples of ice prepared for each group of students. Also, leave out enough water for a few hours prior to beginning this experiment so it becomes room temperature.

Phases of Water (cont.)

Science Experiment Procedure

1. Make a Phases of Water data table similar to the one in Table 3-1. You can also make copies of the data table template shown on page 27.

State of Matter (Water)	Temperature (degrees F)	Temperature (degrees C)
Solid (ice)		
Liquid (room temperature)		
Gas (water vapor)		

Table 3-1

2. Place the Fahrenheit thermometer on the ice cube and leave it there for one minute using the stopwatch. Record the temperature in the data table.

3. Repeat the same procedure using the Celsius thermometer and record the temperature in the data table.

4. Next, use both thermometers to record the temperature of the room-temperature water.

5. Finally, with help from the teacher, use both thermometers to take the temperature of boiling water. Don't forget your oven mitt!

6. Record the data in the State of Matter data sheet and the experiment is complete!

Brainstorming

Once the class has completed the exploration of different forms water can assume (states of matter), instruct students to compare their temperatures with other groups. Then ask the class to come up with explanations of why some groups have different temperatures. Have them come up with ways to make their temperature data more accurate.

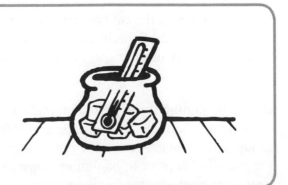

Phases of Water *(cont.)*

Science Experiment Procedure *(cont.)*

Phases of Water Data Table Templates

State of Matter (water)	Temperature (degrees F)	Temperature (degrees C)
Solid (ice)		
Liquid (room temperature)		
Gas (water vapor)		

State of Matter (water)	Temperature (degrees F)	Temperature (degrees C)
Solid (ice)		
Liquid (room temperature)		
Gas (water vapor)		

Phases of Water (cont.)

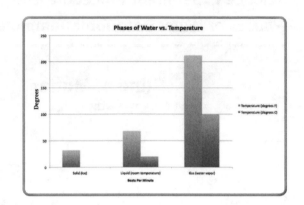

Technology Learning Objectives

At the end of this lesson, students will:

1. Know the various terms associated with spreadsheets including rows, columns, and cells.
2. Enter data into a spreadsheet.
3. Adjust the width of a selected column.
4. Change the alignment of data within a cell.
5. Change the style of data within a cell.
6. Create and format a column graph from data entered within a spreadsheet.

Teacher Note

The technology portion of this activity is written for MS Excel 2010 but can be completed using most spreadsheet and word processing software versions like Open Office, Google Docs, and iWorks with minimal modification.

Technology Procedure

1. Open a new spreadsheet document. Spreadsheets are made up of *columns* that are identified by letters (A, B, C, etc.) and *rows* that are identified by numbers (1, 2, 3, etc.).
2. The location within a spreadsheet where a column meets a row is called a *cell* and is identified by both a letter and number (Figure 3-1).

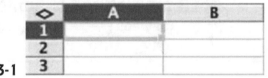

Figure 3-1

3. Click into cell **A1** and type in the label: "State of Matter (water)." Hit the **Tab** key on the keyboard to bring you over to cell **B1** and type in the label: "Temperature (degrees F)."
4. Hit the **Tab** key to move you over to cell **C1** and type in the label: "Temperature (degrees C)."
5. Now widen each column within the spreadsheet to make the labels fit. To do this, move the cursor to the line between columns A and B (Figure 3-2) and click and drag it to the right until the column is wide enough to fit the entire label. Repeat the same procedure for columns B and C.

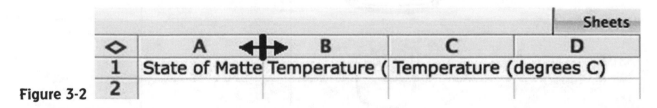

Figure 3-2

Phases of Water *(cont.)*

Technology Procedure *(cont.)*

6. Next, click and drag over the three column labels and use the **Bold** button on the toolbar to make the column titles bold (Figure 3-3).

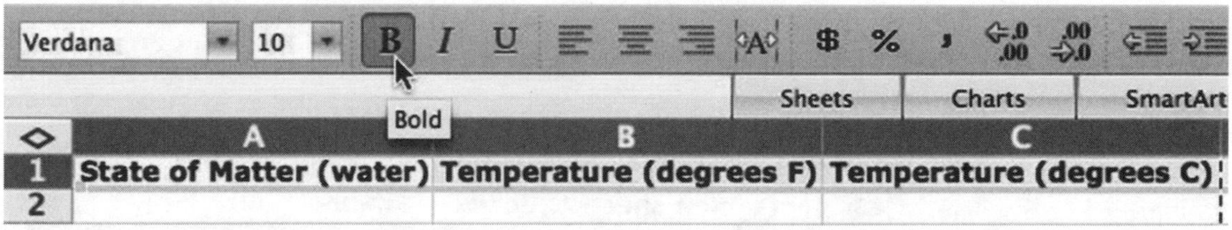

Figure 3-3

7. Now enter the data into the spreadsheet.

8. Next, highlight all the data in the spreadsheet by clicking and dragging over it. Then use the **Align Center** button to center the data (Figure 3-4).

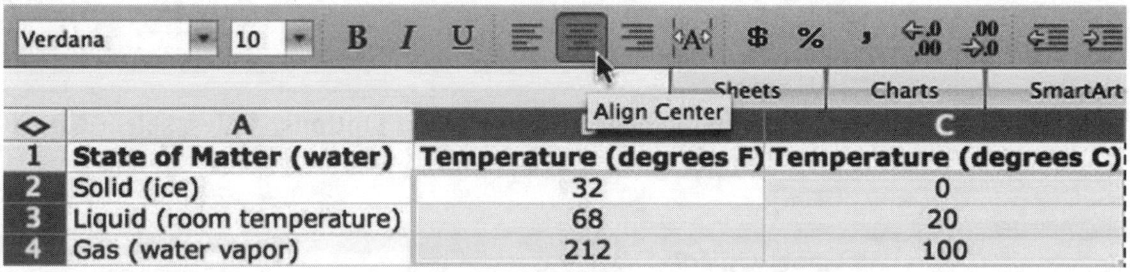

Figure 3-4

9. Now you will use the *States of Matter* data to create a column graph. Click and drag over all the data and labels in the spreadsheet to highlight them. Then go to the **Insert** menu, choose **Chart**, and select **Column** (Figure 3-5).

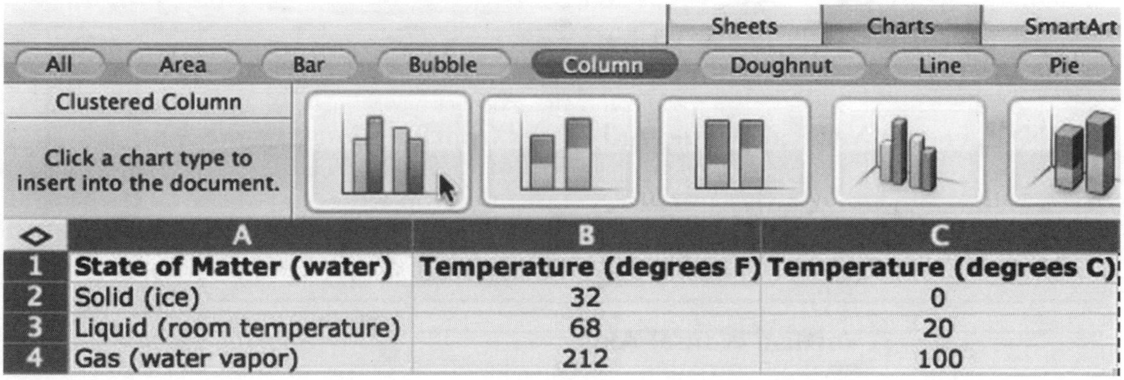

Figure 3-5

Phases of Water (cont.)

Technology Procedure (cont.)

10. Next, you will display the graph to fit on one page. Go to the **Chart** menu and select **Move Chart**, then choose **New Sheet** (Figure 3-6). Click **OK**.

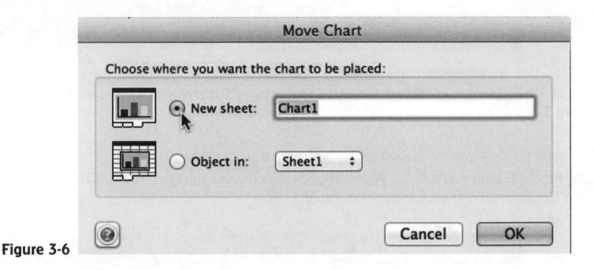

Figure 3-6

11. Now you will add a title to the chart. Under **Chart Options, Titles**, select **Chart Title** and enter: "Phases of Water vs. Temperature" (Figure 3-7).

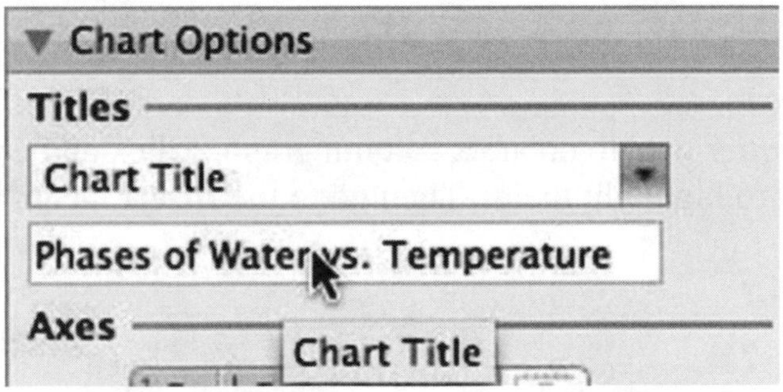

Figure 3-7

12. Next, choose **Vertical (Value) Axis** under **Chart Options** (Figure 3-8).

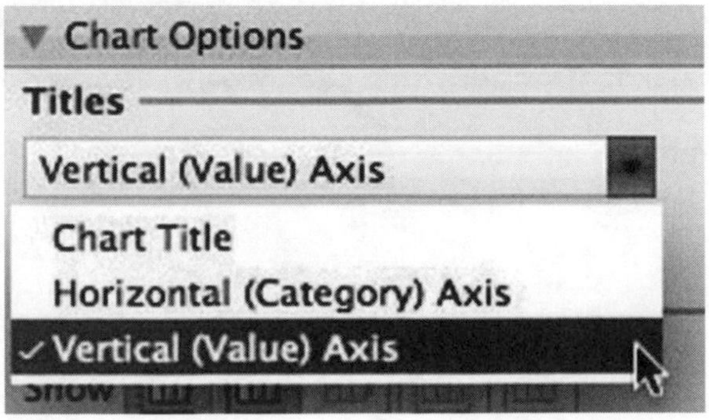

Figure 3-8

Phases of Water *(cont.)*

Technology Procedure *(cont.)*

13. In the **Vertical (Value) Axis** box type the label: "Degrees."
14. Your chart is now complete. **Save** and **Print**. It should look similar to the one in Figure 3-9.

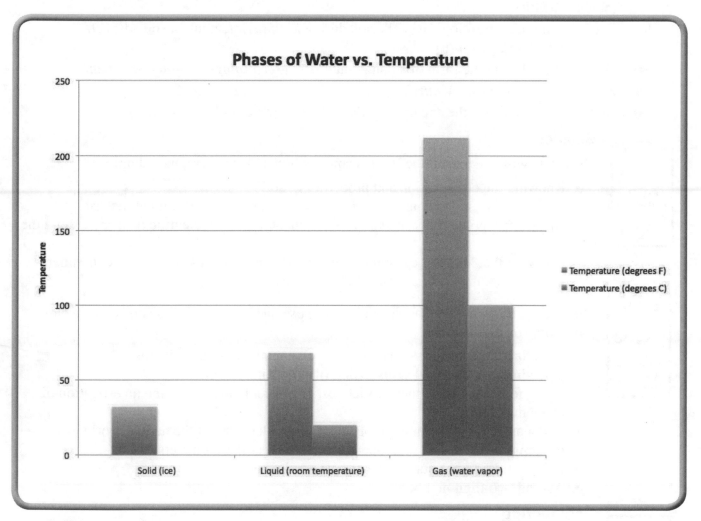

Figure 3-9

Soil Composition

STEM Project Overview

Students will collaborate to:

➥ Collect soil samples and analyze them for their sand, silt, and clay content. (***Science/Math***)

➥ Enter the Soil Composition data collected during an experiment into a spreadsheet. (***Science/Technology/Math***)

➥ Display their data in the form of a doughnut chart. (***Technology/Engineering/Math***)

➥ Evaluate their findings. (***Math***)

➥ Brainstorm to improve the experimentation process. (***Science/Engineering***)

Science

Students will understand the Earth's composition and structure, including:

- Knowing the composition and properties of soil
- Knowing that soil is composed of weathered rock, plant and animal material
- Using appropriate tools and simple equipment to gather scientific data and extend the senses
- Knowing that learning can come from careful observations and simple experiments

Math

Students will use mathematical analysis to pose questions, seek answers, and develop solutions, including:

- Selecting the appropriate operation to solve mathematical problems
- Applying mathematical skills to describe the natural world
- Using representations such as pictures, charts, and tables from the investigation of mathematical ideas
- Using appropriate scientific tools to solve problems about the natural world
- Relating measurement of temperature to different thermometers
- Using a ruler to measure to the nearest centimeter
- Adding two-digit numbers

Engineering

Students will use engineering design to pose questions, seek answers, and develop solutions, including:

- Proposing alternative solutions for procedures
- Using a variety of verbal and graphic techniques to present conclusions
- Identifying simple problems and solutions
- Understanding troubleshooting procedures

Technology

Students will know the characteristics, uses, and basic features of computer software programs, including:

- Knowing the common features and uses of spreadsheets
- Using spreadsheet software to update, add and delete data, and to produce charts

Soil Composition

Materials

- Mason jar with lid (per group)
- rulers (cm)
- soil samples
- shovels
- water (sink or bucket)

Vocabulary

clay—weathered rock smaller than silt

inorganic—non-living

loam—a soil that is good for plant growth and contains nearly equal parts of sand, silt, and clay

mineral—a solid, inorganic material that makes up rocks

organic—living

sand—weathered rock smaller than 0.2 cm and larger than silt

silt—weathered rock smaller than sand and larger than clay

soil—a mixture of organic material, minerals, air, and water important for plant growth

Background

Before beginning this experiment, locate an area near the school where you can take the students to collect their own soil samples. If you can't take the class outside to collect soil, you can bring in soil in buckets for the class to sample, or ask students to bring samples from home. **Make sure to only use soil collected from outdoors. Do not use bagged potting soil.** Also, when you are getting the soil, try not to disturb it by crushing it into small pieces. The lumps will give you better results.

Discuss what soil is made of. Explain that the minerals in soil are classified by their size as being either *sand, silt,* or *clay,* which affects how plants will grow in a soil. Mention that a good soil for plant growth contains nearly equal parts of sand, silt, and clay. Also, too much clay in a soil makes it difficult for water to enter a soil and too much sand doesn't hold enough water in a soil.

Science Experiment Procedure

1. Make a Soil Composition data table similar to the one in Table 4-1. You can also make copies of the data table template shown on page 35.

Soil Composition	
Soil Mineral	**Thickness (cm)**
Clay	
Silt	
Sand	
Total Thickness	

Table 4-1

Soil Composition *(cont.)*

Science Experiment Procedure *(cont.)*

2. Fill the Mason jar approximately 2/3 full with a soil sample collected either outdoors or from the bucket provided by the teacher.

3. Bring the jar over to the sink (or bucket of water) and carefully fill it with water, up to about 1 inch from the top.

4. Carefully place the lid onto the jar and secure it tightly.

5. With help from the teacher, shake the jar to completely mix the water and soil together.

6. Once the soil and water are completely mixed, place the jar somewhere within the classroom to settle for at least 24 hours. Do not disturb the jar during this time.

7. After 24 hours, carefully observe what happened inside without disturbing the jar.

8. The soil should now be separated into four distinct layers. Floating at the top is the organic layer. The sand should be the bottom layer, followed by silt. A layer of clay should be visible on top of the silt.

9. With help from the teacher, use a ruler to measure the thickness of each individual layer of sand, silt, and clay. Record the measurements in the data table.

10. Finally, determine the sum of all three layers of minerals (clay, silt, and sand) within the jar and record in the data table.

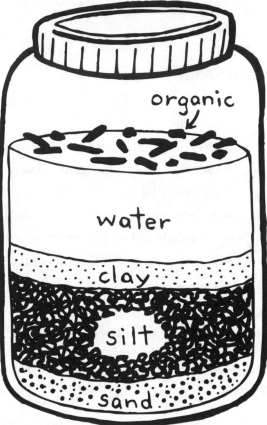

Brainstorming

Once the class has completed the activity, ask students if they think all soils contain the same percentages of sand, silt, and clay.

Challenge the class to come up with an experiment to determine how sand, silt, and clay affect how water moves through a soil. One idea is to fill three separate containers, one with sand, one silt, and one with clay, then have the class time how long it takes a specific volume of water to infiltrate each of them.

Soil Composition *(cont.)*

Science Experiment Procedure *(cont.)*

Soil Composition Data Table Templates

Soil Composition	
Soil Mineral	**Thickness (cm)**
Clay	
Silt	
Sand	
Total Thickness	

Soil Composition	
Soil Mineral	**Thickness (cm)**
Clay	
Silt	
Sand	
Total Thickness	

Soil Composition	
Soil Mineral	**Thickness (cm)**
Clay	
Silt	
Sand	
Total Thickness	

Soil Composition *(cont.)*

Technology Learning Objectives

At the end of this lesson, students will:

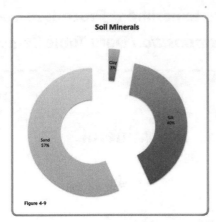

Soil Minerals

Figure 4-9

1. Know the various terms associated with spreadsheets, including rows, columns, and cells.
2. Enter data into a spreadsheet.
3. Adjust the width of a selected column.
4. Change the alignment of data within a cell.
5. Change the style of data within a cell.
6. Create and format a doughnut chart from data entered within a spreadsheet.

Teacher Note

The technology portion of this activity is written for MS Excel 2010 but can be completed using most spreadsheet and word processing software versions like Open Office, Google Docs, and iWorks with minimal modification.

Technology Procedure

1. Open a new spreadsheet document. Spreadsheets are made up of *columns* that are identified by letters (A, B, C, etc.) and *rows* that are identified by numbers (1, 2, 3, etc.).
2. The location within a spreadsheet where a column meets a row is called a *cell* and is identified by both a letter and number (Figure 4-1).

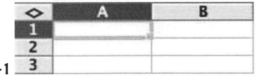

Figure 4-1

3. Click into cell **A1** and type in the label: "Soil Mineral." Hit the **Tab** key on the keyboard to bring you over to cell **B1** and type in the label: "Thickness (cm)."
4. Next, click and drag over the two column labels and use the **Bold** button on the toolbar to make the column titles bold (Figure 4-2).

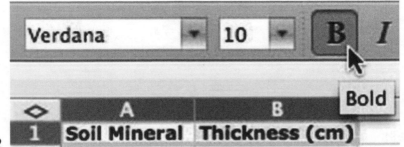

Figure 4-2

Soil Composition *(cont.)*

Technology Procedure *(cont.)*

5. Next, enter the data you gathered on the thickness of each mineral layer, along with the sum of the total depth of the mineral layers from the data sheet, into the spreadsheet (Figure 4-3).

	A	B
1	**Soil Mineral**	**Thickness (cm)**
2	Clay	1
3	Silt	4
4	Sand	6
5	Total Thickness	11

Figure 4-3

6. Highlight all of the data within the spreadsheet by clicking and dragging over it. Then use the **Center Align** button to center the data in each cell (Figure 4-4).

Verdana	10	**B**	*I*	U				

Align Center

	A	B	C
1	**Soil Mineral**	**Thickness (cm)**	
2	Clay	1	
3	Silt	4	
4	Sand	6	

Figure 4-4

7. Next you will make a doughnut chart. Click into cell **A1**, then click and drag over all the data except the "Total Depth" row to highlight it (Figure 4-5).

	A	B	C
1	**Soil Mineral**	**Thickness (cm)**	
2	Clay	1	
3	Silt	4	
4	Sand	6	
5	Total Thickness	11	
6			

Figure 4-5

8. With the data still highlighted, go to the **Insert** menu, select **Chart**, and choose **Exploded Doughnut** (Figure 4-6).

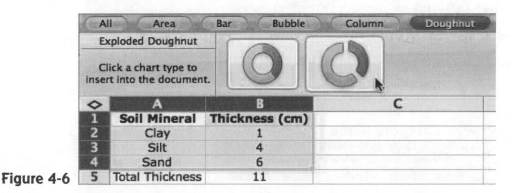

All	Area	Bar	Bubble	Column	Doughnut

Exploded Doughnut

Click a chart type to insert into the document.

	A	B	C
1	**Soil Mineral**	**Thickness (cm)**	
2	Clay	1	
3	Silt	4	
4	Sand	6	
5	Total Thickness	11	

Figure 4-6

Soil Composition *(cont.)*

Technology Procedure *(cont.)*

9. Next, you will display the graph to fit on one page. Go to the **Chart** menu and select "Move Chart," then choose "New Sheet." Click **OK**.

10. Now you will change the title of the chart. Under **Chart Options, Titles**, select **Chart Title** and enter "Soil Minerals" (Figure 4-7).

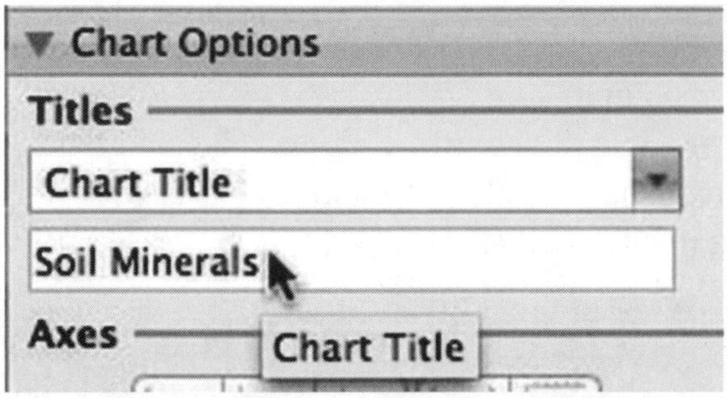

Figure 4-7

11. Next, you will add labels to the doughnut chart. Select **Labels,** then **Category Name and Percent** (Figure 4-8).

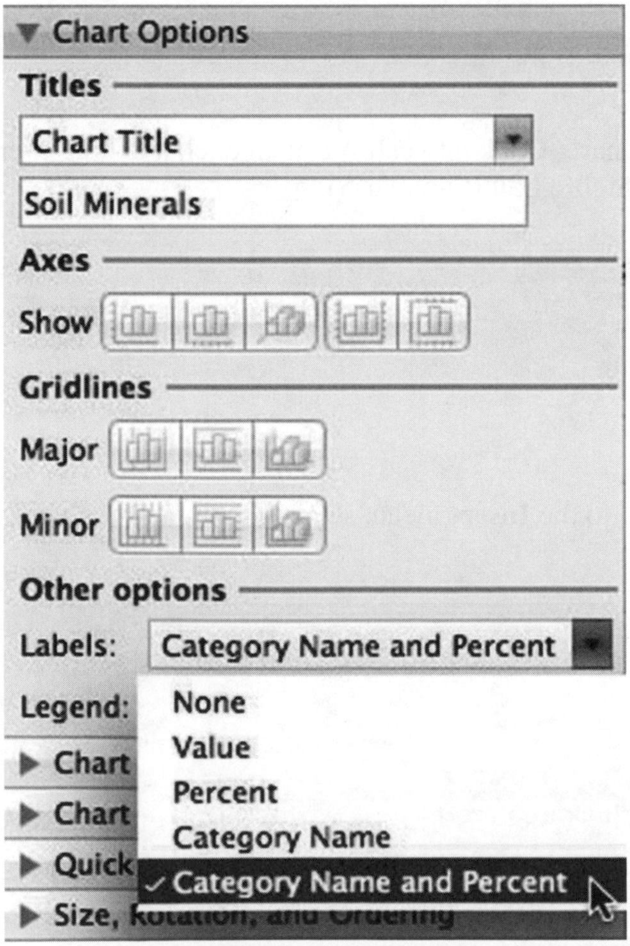

Figure 4-8

Soil Composition *(cont.)*

Technology Procedure *(cont.)*

12. Your chart is now complete. **Save** and **Print**. It should look similar to the one in Figure 4-9.

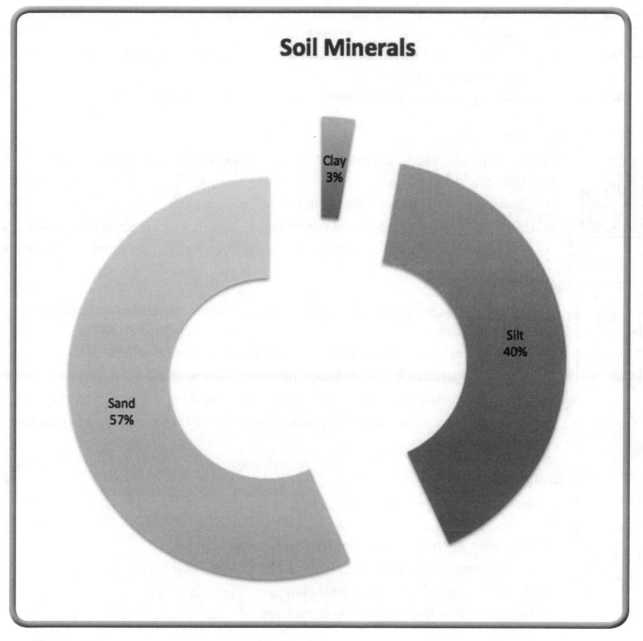

Figure 4-9

Plant Growth Rate

STEM Project Overview

Students will collaborate to:

➡ Observe how a plant's growth is affected by light. *(Science/Math)*

➡ Enter the Plant Growth Rate data collected during an experiment into a spreadsheet. *(Technology/Math)*

➡ Display their data in the form of a bar graph. *(Technology/Engineering/Math)*

➡ Evaluate their findings. *(Math)*

➡ Brainstorm to improve the experimentation process. *(Science/Engineering)*

Science

Students will understand the relationships among organisms and their physical environment, including:

• Knowing that a plant's environment will affect its growth

• Using appropriate tools and simple equipment to gather scientific data and extend the senses

• Knowing that learning can come from careful observations and simple experiments

Math

Students will use mathematical analysis to pose questions, seek answers, and develop solutions, including:

• Selecting the appropriate operation to solve mathematical problems

• Applying mathematical skills to describe the natural world

• Using appropriate scientific tools to solve problems about the natural world

• Using representations such as pictures, charts, and tables from the investigation of mathematical ideas

Engineering

Students will use engineering design to pose questions, seek answers, and develop solutions, including:

• Proposing alternative solutions for procedures

• Using a variety of verbal and graphic techniques to present conclusions

• Identifying simple problems and solutions

• Understanding troubleshooting procedures

Technology

Students will know the characteristics, uses, and basic features of computer software programs, including:

• Knowing the common features and uses of spreadsheets

• Using spreadsheet software to update, add and delete data, and to produce charts

Plant Growth Rate

Materials

- 2 plant pots or plastic containers (per group)
- 2 bean seeds (per group)
- magic markers
- masking tape
- potting soil
- rulers (cm)
- grow light (optional)

Vocabulary

germinate—the sprouting of a plant from a seed

leaf—the part of a plant that produces food

roots—the underground part of a plant that takes in water and nutrients

seed—the part of a plant that forms a new plant

stem—the stalk of a plant that supports leaves and flowers

Background

Before beginning this experiment, review or introduce the basic life cycle of a plant going from seed, germination, growth, flowering, and reproduction.

This experiment requires one of the two plants to receive an ample amount of sunlight throughout the day. If a sunny window is not available, you may wish to place the plants that require adequate sunlight under a grow light.

Science Experiment Procedure

1. Make a Plant Growth Rate data table similar to the one in Table 5-1. You can also make copies of the data table template shown on page 43.

Plant Growth Rate		
Day	Height (cm) of Bean Plant in Full Light	Height (cm) of Bean Plant in Low Light
1		
2		
3		
4		
5		

Table 5-1

Plant Growth Rate *(cont.)*

Science Experiment Procedure *(cont.)*

2. Fill 2 small plant pots with soil.

3. Label one pot "Full Light" and the other pot "Low Light," using masking tape. Include the name (or group name) on each pot's label.

4. Plant one seed in each pot, about 2 cm deep.

5. Place one pot in full light and the other pot in a low light area.

6. Water each pot with enough water to moisten the soil.

7. Observe the pots each day. Once the seeds begin to sprout, use a ruler to determine the height of each plant. Measure the plants each day.

8. To determine the height of each plant, measure the distance from the top of the soil to the point on the stem where the first set of leaves branches off.

9. Record the first measurements in the data table under "Day 1."

10. Continue to measure the height of each plant for a period of one week.

Brainstorming

Before the plants sprout, ask the class to predict what will happen with the growth of each plant. Once the class has completed the activity, discuss the results of their experiment. Ask them how the results of their experiment compared to their predictions.

Challenge the class to design a method for them to place both pots in the full light area and reduce the amount of light that one pot receives. Some ideas may include using a screen or colored cellophane to reduce the light that the low-light plant receives.

Plant Growth Rate (cont.)

Science Experiment Procedure (cont.)

Plant Growth Rate Data Table Templates

	Plant Growth Rate	
Day	**Height (cm) of Bean Plant in Full Light**	**Height (cm) of Bean Plant in Low Light**
1		
2		
3		
4		
5		

	Plant Growth Rate	
Day	**Height (cm) of Bean Plant in Full Light**	**Height (cm) of Bean Plant in Low Light**
1		
2		
3		
4		
5		

Plant Growth Rate *(cont.)*

Technology Learning Objectives

At the end of this lesson, students will:

1. Know the various terms associated with spreadsheets, including rows, columns, and cells.
2. Enter data into a spreadsheet.
3. Adjust the width of a selected column.
4. Change the alignment of data within a cell.
5. Change the style of data within a cell.
6. Create and format a 3D area chart from data entered within a spreadsheet.

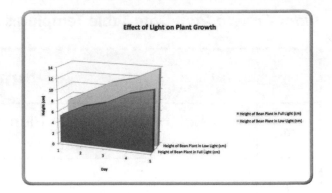

Teacher Note

The technology portion of this activity is written for MS Excel 2010 but can be completed using most spreadsheet and word processing software versions like Open Office, Google Docs, and iWorks with minimal modification.

Technology Procedure

1. Open a new spreadsheet document. Spreadsheets are made up of *columns* that are identified by letters (A, B, C, etc.) and *rows* that are identified by numbers (1, 2, 3, etc.).
2. The location within a spreadsheet where a column meets a row is called a *cell* and is identified by both a letter and number (Figure 5-1).

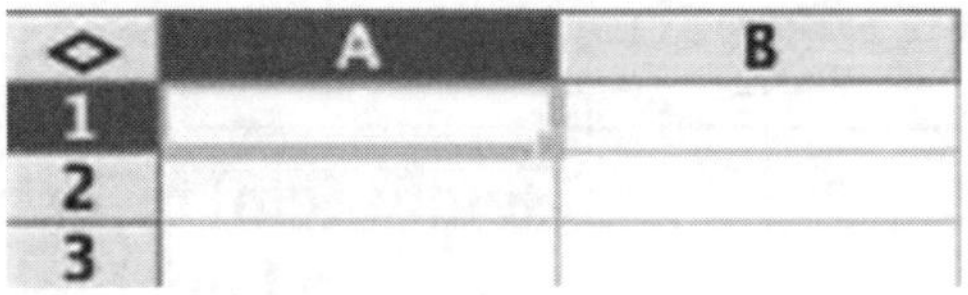

Figure 5-1

3. Click into cell **A1** and type in the label: "Day." Hit the **Tab** key on the keyboard to bring you over to cell **B1** and type in the label: "Height of Bean Plant in Full Light (cm)."
4. Next, you will have to widen column B so that its label fits within the cell. To do this, use the mouse to move the cursor over the line between column B and C at the top of the spreadsheet. Then click and drag it to the right until the column is wide enough for the label to fit (Figure 5-2).

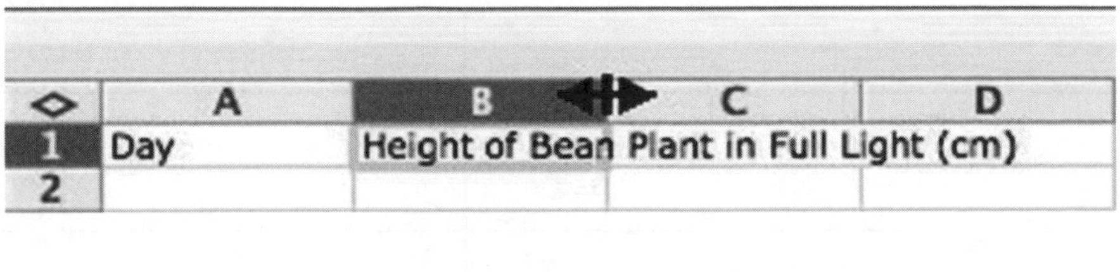

Figure 5-2

Plant Growth Rate (cont.)

Technology Procedure (cont.)

5. Hit the **Tab** key on the keyboard to move over into cell **C1** and type in the label: "Height of Bean Plant in Low Light (cm)."

6. Widen column C so the label fits within it.

7. Next, click and drag over all three labels to highlight them and use the **Align Center** button to center them (Figure 5-3).

Figure 5-3

8. Next, enter the data you gathered on the growth of each plant into the spreadsheet (Figure 5-4).

	A	B	C
1	Day	Height of Bean Plant in Full Light (cm)	Height of Bean Plant in Low Light (cm)
2	1	5	7
3	2	7	9
4	3	8	11
5	4	10	12
6	5	11	14

Figure 5-4

9. Once you have entered all of the height data, click and drag over it to highlight it, and center it using the **Align Center** button.

10. Click into cell **A1**, then go to the **Insert** menu, and choose **Chart**.

11. Select "3D Area" (Figure 5-5).

Figure 5-5

12. Next, you will display the graph to fit on one page. Go to the **Chart** menu and select "Move Chart," then choose "New Sheet." Click **OK**.

Plant Growth Rate *(cont.)*

Technology Procedure *(cont.)*

13. First, click on the area in the chart labeled "Day" to highlight it (Figure 5-6) and hit delete on the keyboard to remove it from the chart.

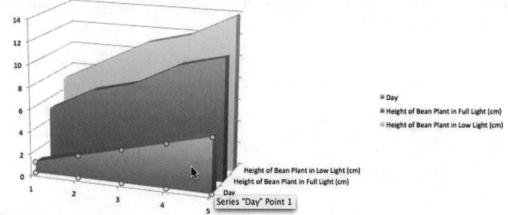

Figure 5-6

14. Now, click into the **Chart Title** box, under **Chart Options, Titles** and enter the following title: "Effect of Light on Plant Growth" (Figure 5-7).

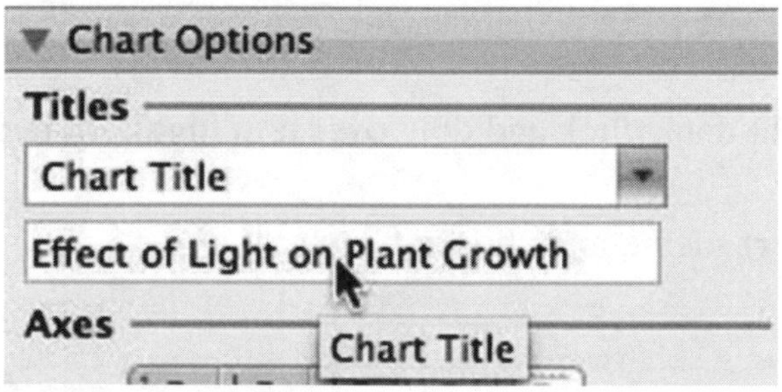

Figure 5-7

15. Next, under **Chart Options, Titles**, select **Horizontal (Category) Axis** (Figure 5-8) and type in "Day."

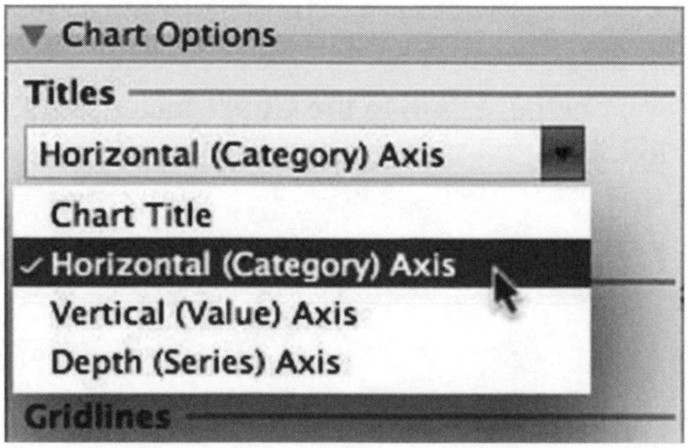

Figure 5-8

16. Now select the **Vertical (Value) Axis** and type in "Height (cm)."

Plant Growth Rate *(cont.)*

Technology Procedure *(cont.)*

17. Your chart is now complete. **Save** and **Print**. It should look similar to the one in Figure 5-9.

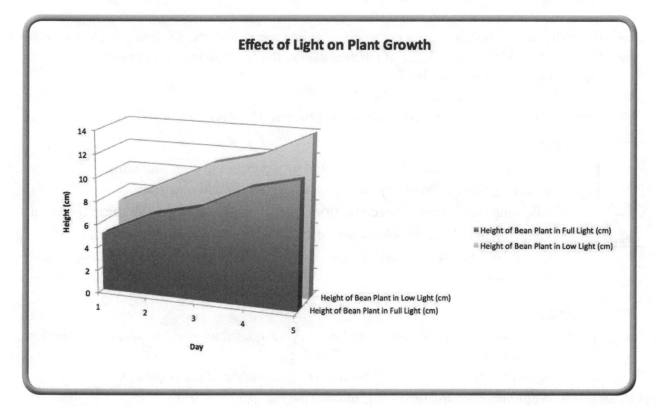

Figure 5-9

Mass and Volume of Objects

STEM Project Overview

Students will collaborate to:

➡ Record the mass and volume of different items of similar size. *(Science/Math)*

➡ Enter the data collected during an experiment into a spreadsheet. *(Science/Technology/Math)*

➡ Display their Mass and Volume of Objects data in the form of a column graph. *(Technology/Engineering/Math)*

➡ Evaluate their findings. *(Science/Math)*

➡ Brainstorm to improve the experimentation process. *(Science/Engineering)*

Science

Students will understand the structure and properties of matter, including:

• Knowing that different objects are made up of different materials

• Knowing that learning can come from careful observations and simple experiments

• Knowing that different objects have different observable properties like size and weight

• Using appropriate tools and simple equipment to gather scientific data and extend the senses

Math

Students will use mathematical analysis to pose questions, seek answers, and develop solutions, including:

• Selecting the appropriate operation to solve mathematical problems

• Applying mathematical skills to describe the natural world

• Subtracting two-digit numbers

• Using appropriate scientific tools to solve problems about the natural world

• Using representations such as pictures, charts, and tables from the investigation of mathematical ideas

Engineering

Students will use engineering design to pose questions, seek answers, and develop solutions, including:

• Proposing alternative solutions for procedures

• Using a variety of verbal and graphic techniques to present conclusions

• Identifying simple problems and solutions

• Devising ways to determine the volume of a solid object

Technology

Students will know the characteristics, uses, and basic features of computer software programs, including:

• Knowing the common features and uses of spreadsheets

• Using spreadsheet software to update, add and delete data, and to produce charts

Mass and Volume of Objects *(cont.)*

Materials

- 1" cube of metal (per group)
- 1" cube of plastic (per group)
- 1" cube of wood (per group)
- 250 ml graduated cylinder (per group)
- large paper clip (per group)
- scale or balance
- scrap piece of paper (per group)

Vocabulary

mass—the amount of matter in an object

volume—the amount of space an object takes up

displacement—the change in the volume of water when something is placed within it

Background

Before beginning this experiment, obtain sets of three cubes. The cubes should all be the same volume, and should be made of wood, steel, and PVC plastic. These sets are commonly used in middle or high school science programs. They are commonly referred to as "density cubes." Also, make sure that the cubes you will be using in this activity will fit within the graduated cylinders.

Demonstrate how to carefully use a graduated cylinder and explain the water-displacement method that will be used to determine the volume of each object. To do this, fill a graduated cylinder with a known volume of water; this is the *start* volume. Then carefully slide the object into the graduated cylinder and record the volume in the graduated cylinder. This is the *end* volume. To determine the volume of the object, subtract the start volume from the end volume.

Science Experiment Procedure

1. Make a Mass and Volume of Objects data table similar to the one in Table 6-1. You can also make copies of the data table template shown on page 51.

Mass and Volume of Objects		
Object	**Mass (grams)**	**Volume (ml)**
Wood		
Plastic		
Metal		

Table 6-1

Mass and Volume of Objects *(cont.)*

Science Experiment Procedure *(cont.)*

2. Gather the three 1" cubes and use a scale or balance to determine their mass in grams.

3. Record the mass of each cube in the Mass and Volume of Objects data table.

4. Now fill the graduated cylinder with 100 ml of water. This is the start volume.

5. Record the start volume on a scrap piece of paper.

6. Carefully tilt the graduated cylinder a little to the side and slide the metal cube into it. This is the end volume.

7. Record the end volume on the scrap piece of paper.

8. Now subtract the start volume from the end volume. The difference between the two volumes is the volume of the cube.

9. Record the volume of the metal cube in the data table.

10. Carefully empty the water from the graduated cylinder into the sink (or bucket) and retrieve the metal cube.

11. Next, use the same procedure to determine the volume of the plastic cube and record it in the data table.

12. Now you will determine the volume of the wood cube. Because the wood will float on the water, you will need to use a paperclip to hold it down under the water within the graduated cylinder.

13. With help from the teacher, unfold the paperclip to form a straight wire.

14. Fill the graduated cylinder with 100 ml of water.

15. Place the wood cube in the graduated cylinder and use the paperclip to hold it down under the water.

16. Subtract the start volume from the end volume and record it in the data table.

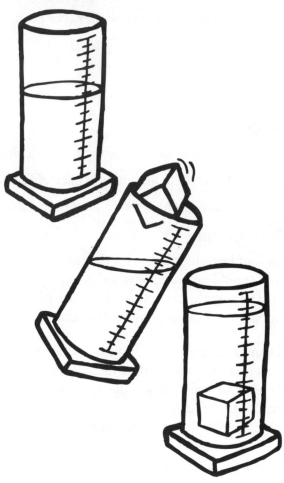

Brainstorming

Once the class has completed the activity, instruct students to compare their data with other groups. Then ask the class why it was important to determine the mass of the cubes before they were put in water. *(Because water has mass and will increase the mass of the cube.)*

Challenge the class to design a container that can be used to determine the volume of liquids.

Mass and Volume of Objects *(cont.)*

Science Experiment Procedure *(cont.)*

Mass and Volume of Objects **Data Table Templates**

Mass and Volume of Objects

Object		Mass (grams)	Volume (ml)
Wood			
Plastic			
Metal			

Mass and Volume of Objects

Object		Mass (grams)	Volume (ml)
Wood			
Plastic			
Metal			

Mass and Volume of Objects

Object		Mass (grams)	Volume (ml)
Wood			
Plastic			
Metal			

Mass and Volume of Objects *(cont.)*

Technology Learning Objectives

At the end of this lesson, students will:

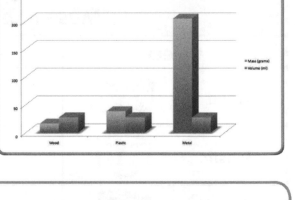

Mass and Volume of Different Objects

1. Know the various terms associated with spreadsheets, including rows, columns, and cells.
2. Enter data into a spreadsheet.
3. Adjust the width of a selected column.
4. Change the alignment of data within a cell.
5. Change the style of data within a cell.
6. Create and format a 3D clustered column graph from data entered within a spreadsheet.

> **Teacher Note**
>
> The technology portion of this activity is written for MS Excel 2010 but can be completed using most spreadsheet and word processing software versions like Open Office, Google Docs, and iWorks with minimal modification.

Technology Procedure

1. Open a new spreadsheet document. Spreadsheets are made up of *columns* that are identified by letters (A, B, C, etc.) and *rows* that are identified by numbers (1, 2, 3, etc.).
2. The location within a spreadsheet where a column meets a row is called a *cell* and is identified by both a letter and number (Figure 6-1).

Figure 6-1

3. Click into cell **A1** and type in the label: "Object." Hit the **Tab** key on the keyboard to bring you over to cell **B1** and type in the label: "Mass (grams)."
4. Hit the **Tab** key to move you over to cell **C1** and type in the label: "Volume (ml)."
5. Next, click and drag over the three column labels and use the **Bold** button on the toolbar to make the column titles bold (Figure 6-2).

Figure 6-2

	A	B		D
1	Object	Mass (grams	Volume (ml)	
2				

Mass and Volume of Objects *(cont.)*

Technology Procedures *(cont.)*

6. Take the cursor and bring it between columns B and C, then click and drag it to the right to widen the column so the label in cell **B1** fits (Figure 6-3).

Figure 6-3

7. Now enter the data into the spreadsheet.

8. Next, highlight all the data in the spreadsheet by clicking and dragging over it. Then use the **Align Center** button to center the data (Figure 6-4).

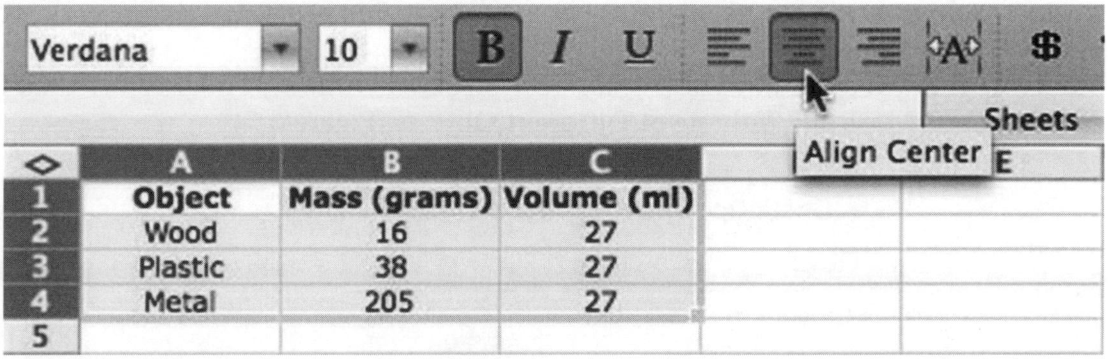

Figure 6-4

9. Now you will use the data to create a column graph. Click and drag over all the data and labels in the spreadsheet to highlight them. Then go to the **Insert** menu, choose **Chart**, and select "3D Clustered Column" (Figure 6-5).

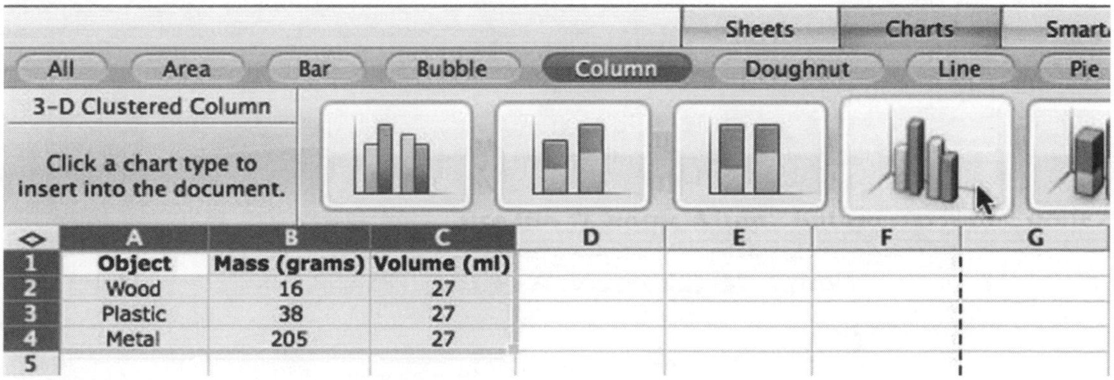

Figure 6-5

Mass and Volume of Objects (cont.)

Technology Procedures (cont.)

10. Next, you will display the graph to fit on one page. Go to the **Chart** menu and select "Move Chart," then choose **New Sheet** (Figure 6-6). Click **OK**.

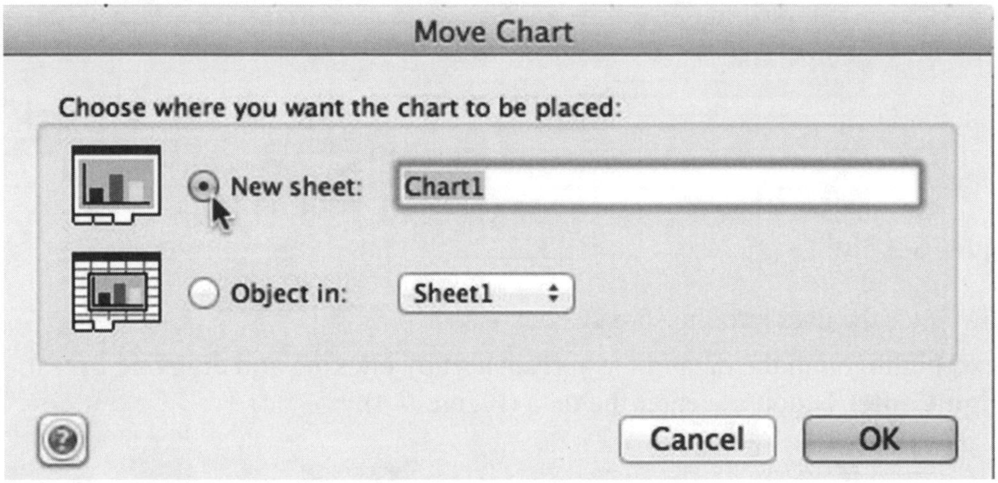

Figure 6-6

11. Now you will add a title to the chart. Under **Chart Options, Titles**, select **Chart Title** and enter the label: **Mass and Volume of Different Objects** (Figure 6-7).

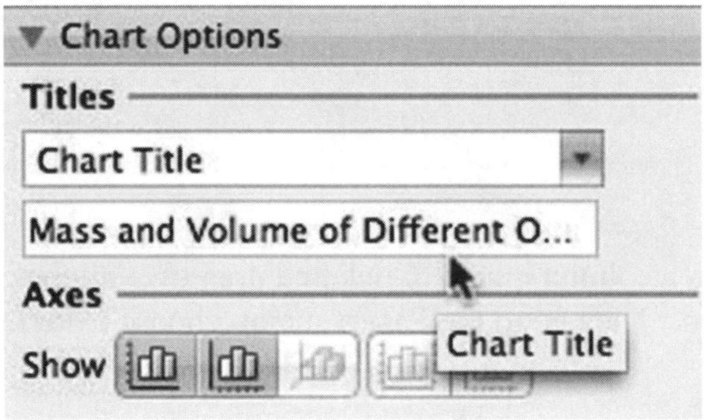

Figure 6-7

12. Next, under **Chart Options, Titles**, select **Horizontal (Category) Axis** (Figure 6-8) and type in the label: "Object."

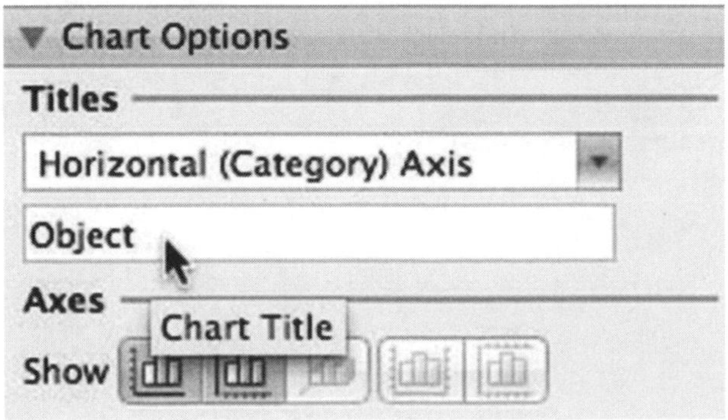

Figure 6-8

Mass and Volume of Objects *(cont.)*

Technology Procedures *(cont.)*

13. Your chart is now complete. **Save** and **Print**. It should look similar to the one in Figure 6-9.

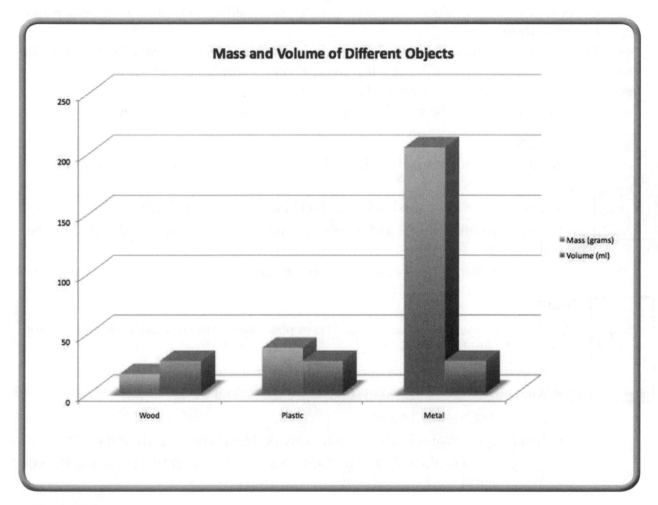

Figure 6-9

Transpiration of Plants

STEM Project Overview

Students will collaborate to:

➡ Observe how environmental conditions affect a plant's ability to photosynthesize or respire. *(Science/Math)*

➡ Enter the data collected during an experiment into a spreadsheet *(Science/Technology/Math)*

➡ Display their data in the form of a line chart. *(Technology/Engineering/Math)*

➡ Evaluate their findings. *(Science/Math)*

➡ Brainstorm to improve the experimentation process. *(Science/Engineering)*

Science

Students will understand the relationships among organisms and their physical environment, including:

- Knowing the basic needs of plants including air, water, and light

- Using appropriate tools and simple equipment to gather scientific data and extend the senses

- Knowing that learning can come from careful observations and simple experiments

Math

Students will use mathematical analysis to pose questions, seek answers, and develop solutions, including:

- Selecting the appropriate operation to solve mathematical problems

- Applying mathematical skills to describe the natural world

- Subtracting two-digit numbers

- Using appropriate scientific tools to solve problems about the natural world

- Using representations such as pictures, charts, and tables from the investigation of mathematical ideas

Engineering

Students will use engineering design to pose questions, seek answers, and develop solutions, including:

- Proposing alternative solutions for procedures

- Using a variety of verbal and graphic techniques to present conclusions

- Identifying simple problems and solutions

- Devising ways to determine the volume of a solid object

Technology

Students will know the characteristics, uses, and basic features of computer software programs, including:

- Knowing the common features and uses of spreadsheets

- Using spreadsheet software to update, add and delete data, and produce charts

Transpiration of Plants *(cont.)*

Materials

- 1 gallon-size plastic re-sealable bag (per group)
- 10 ml graduated cylinder (per group)
- healthy growing deciduous tree with leaves
- masking tape
- plastic wrap
- scale or balance
- scissors
- small rubber band
- toothpick

Vocabulary

transpiration—the movement of water from the ground, into the roots, up through the body of a plant, that evaporates off the leaf surface

evaporation—the phase change from liquid water to water vapor

leaf—the flattened part of a plant where photosynthesis occurs

groundwater—fresh water stored within the ground

Background

Before beginning this activity, locate a healthy tree that will be accessible for students during this experiment. Make certain it is appropriate to conduct experiments using the tree. Broad-leafed deciduous trees like maple trees work best for this activity. Explain to students that this exploration of plant transpiration will include two separate activities.

Science Experiment Procedure

1. Make a simple data table similar to the one in Table 7-1. Or make copies of the more detailed data table template shown on page 60.

2. Use a piece of masking tape to label a plastic bag with the name or the group's name.

3. Use the scale or balance to determine the mass of the gallon-size plastic bag.

4. Record the mass of the empty bag on the same piece of paper containing the data table.

Transpiration of Plants	
Day	**Water Level (ml)**
1	
2	
3	
Total Water Lost	

Table 7-1

Transpiration of Plants *(cont.)*

Science Experiment Procedure *(cont.)*

5. Use another piece of tape to label a 10 ml graduated cylinder with the group's name. This will be used in the second activity. Make sure not to cover the scale (measurements) on the graduated cylinder with the tape.

6. Fill the graduated cylinder with 10 ml of water.

7. With help from the teacher, use a piece of plastic wrap to tightly cover the top of the graduated cylinder.

8. Secure the plastic wrap with a rubber band, so it tightly covers the top of the graduated cylinder.

9. Take the plastic bag, prepared graduated cylinder, and toothpick outside (with the teacher) to complete the two activities.

10. Once outside, with help from the teacher, select a part of the tree that contains 3-4 healthy leaves. Carefully use the plastic bag to cover the leaves. Seal the bag around them by zipping the bag shut. Use tape if necessary.

11. Once the first activity is complete, move to the cylinder.

12. Carefully use the toothpick to poke a tiny hole in the plastic wrap directly over the opening at the top of the graduated cylinder.

13. Select one healthy leaf (with a long stem attached) from the tree and cut it off carefully using the scissors.

14. Quickly place the stem of the leaf through the tiny hole in the plastic wrap into the water of the graduated cylinder. Make sure that the stem is deeply immersed under water.

15. Take the graduated cylinder inside, and place it near a sunny window.

16. Record the level of the water within the graduated cylinder in the data table under "Day 1."

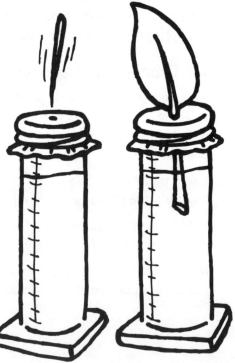

Transpiration of Plants (cont.)

Science Experiment Procedure (cont.)

17. For the next three days, check both the appearance of the bag surrounding the leaves outside, and the water level within the graduated cylinder.

18. Record the water level in the graduated cylinder each day in the data table.

19. After three days, with the help of the teacher, carefully remove the plastic bag from the tree outside.

20. Bring the bag inside, weigh it using a scale or balance, and record it on the data table.

21. Using the data from the data table, subtract the level of the water level on day 3 from the level recorded on day 1. Record the difference in the data table next to "Total Water Loss."

Brainstorming

Once the class has completed the activity, ask students to compare the total water loss by the leaf in the graduated cylinder to the water gained by the bag outside. How are these related?

The loss of the water from the graduated cylinder represents the water gained by the bag, because transpiration takes water from the ground and passes through a plant then back into the atmosphere. Help make the connection that the water lost in the graduated cylinder is lost to the atmosphere and is represented by the water collected in the plastic bag. Remember that one ml of water is equal in mass to one gram.

Also explore the concept of transpiration by plants and how it is an important source of moisture in the atmosphere.

Have the class brainstorm how different factors like exposing the leaf in the cylinder to a light or a fan might have affected the loss of water by the leaf. Extend the activity to include these variables.

Transpiration of Plants *(cont.)*

Science Experiment Procedure *(cont.)*

Transpiration of Plants Data Table Templates

Transpiration of Plants	
Day	**Water Level (ml)**
1	
2	
3	
Total Water Lost	

Mass of empty bag _____

Mass of bag after 3 days around leaves _____

How is the information on the data table related to the information gathered when measuring the 2 bags.

Before covering leaves: _____

After covering leaves: _____

_____

Transpiration of Plants	
Day	**Water Level (ml)**
1	
2	
3	
Total Water Lost	

Mass of empty bag _____

Mass of bag after 3 days around leaves _____

How is the information on the data table related to the information gathered when measuring the 2 bags.

Before covering leaves: _____

After covering leaves: _____

_____

Transpiration of Plants *(cont.)*

Technology Learning Objectives

At the end of this lesson, students will:

1. Know the various terms associated with spreadsheets, including rows, columns, and cells.
2. Enter data into a spreadsheet.
3. Adjust the width of a selected column.
4. Change the alignment of data within a cell.
5. Change the style of data within a cell.
6. Create and format a line chart from data entered within a spreadsheet.

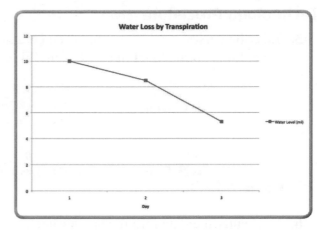

Teacher Note

The technology portion of this activity is written for MS Excel 2010 but can be completed using most spreadsheet and word processing software versions like Open Office, Google Docs, and iWorks with minimal modification.

Technology Procedure

1. Open a new spreadsheet document. Spreadsheets are made up of *columns* that are identified by letters (A, B, C, etc.) and *rows* that are identified by numbers (1, 2, 3, etc.).
2. The location within a spreadsheet where a column meets a row is called a cell and is identified by both a letter and number (Figure 7-1).

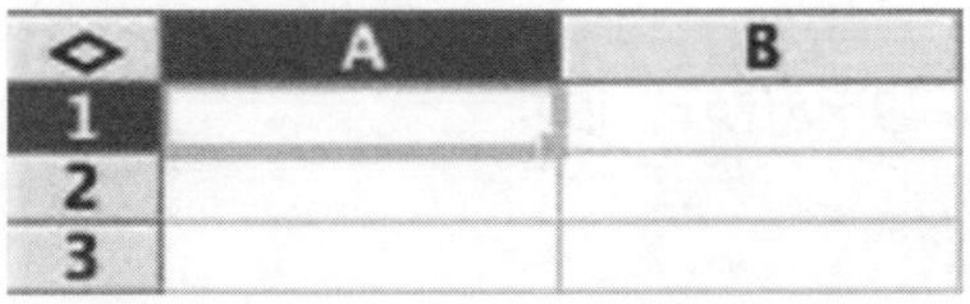

Figure 7-1

3. Click into cell **A1** and type in the label: "Day." Hit the **Tab** key on the keyboard to bring you over to cell **B1** and type in the label: "Water Level (ml)."
4. Next, click and drag over the two column labels. Use the **Bold** button on the toolbar to make the column titles bold (Figure 7-2).

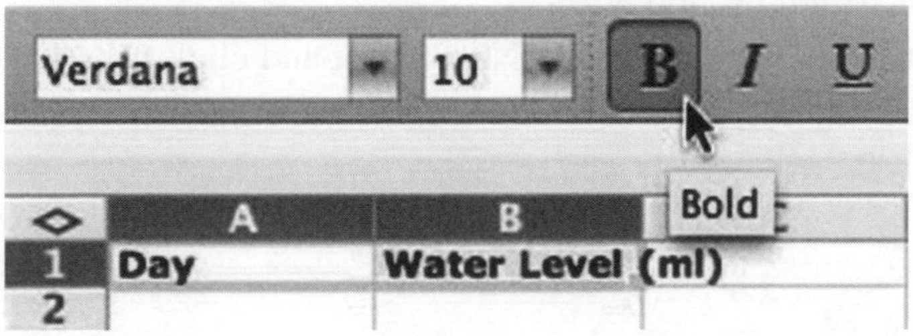

Figure 7-2

Transpiration of Plants *(cont.)*

Technology Procedure *(cont.)*

5. Take the cursor and bring it between columns B and C, then click and drag it to the right to widen the column so the label in cell **B1** fits (Figure 7-3).

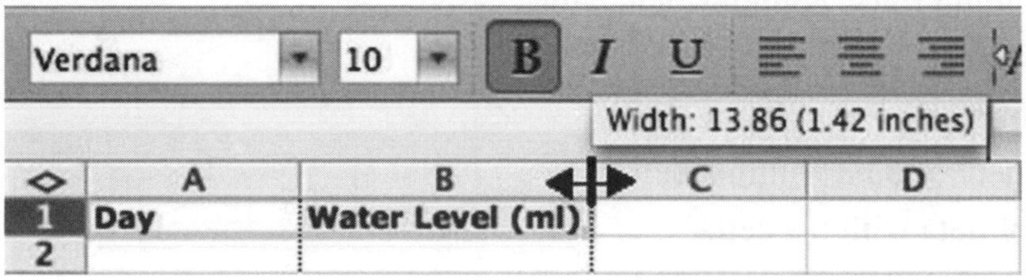

Figure 7-3

6. Now enter the data into the spreadsheet.

7. Next, highlight all the data in the spreadsheet by clicking and dragging over it. Use the **Align Center** button to center the data (Figure 7-4).

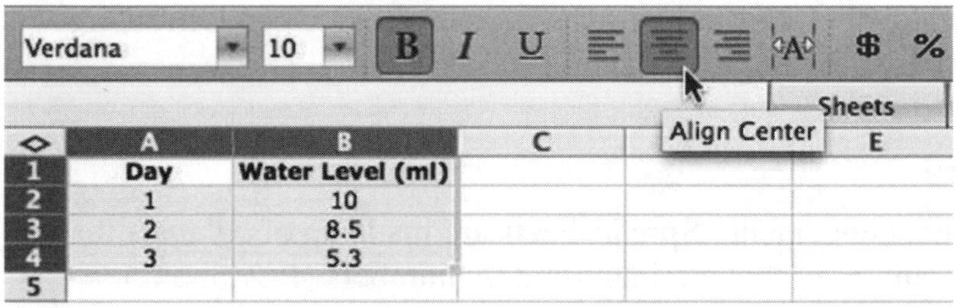

Figure 7-4

8. Now you are going to use the data to create a chart. With the data still highlighted, choose the **Insert** menu, **Chart**, and click on **Line** or **Marked Line** (Figure 7-5).

Figure 7-5

9. Your chart should now appear *within* the spreadsheet.

10. Go to the **Chart** menu, select **Move Chart**, choose **New Sheet** and click **OK** (Figure 7-6).

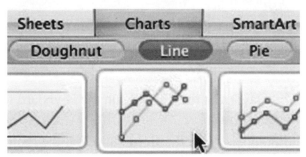

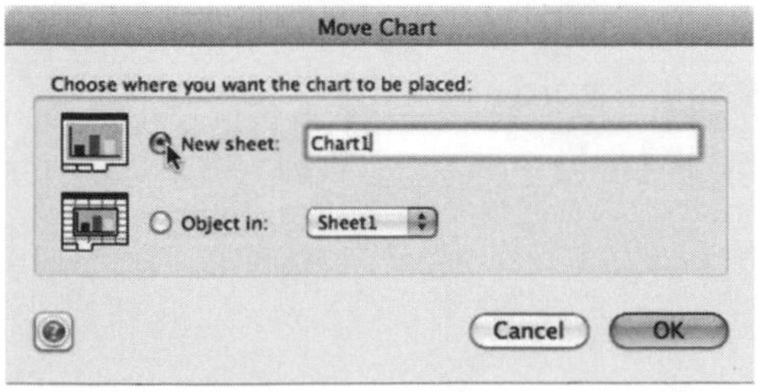

Figure 7-6

Transpiration of Plants *(cont.)*

Technology Procedure *(cont.)*

11. Your chart should now take up the entire page.

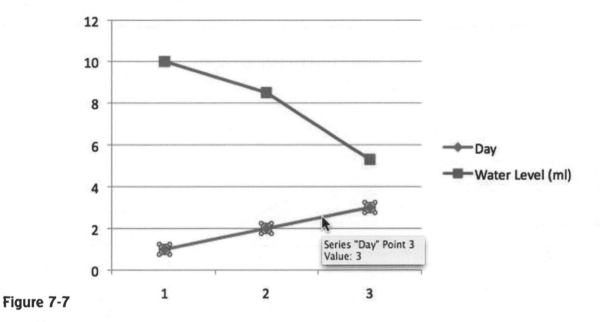

Figure 7-7

12. Right click on the blue line for "Day" and hit **Delete** on the keyboard to remove it from the chart (Figure 7-7).

13. Now you will add a title to the chart. Under **Chart Options, Titles**, select **Chart Title** and enter: "Water Loss by Transpiration" (Figure 7-8).

Figure 7-8

14. Next, under **Chart Options, Titles**, select **Horizontal (Category) Axis** (Figure 7-9) and type in the label: "Day."

Figure 7-9

Transpiration of Plants (cont.)

Technology Procedure (cont.)

15. Your chart is now complete. **Save** and **Print**. It should look similar to the one in Figure 7-10.

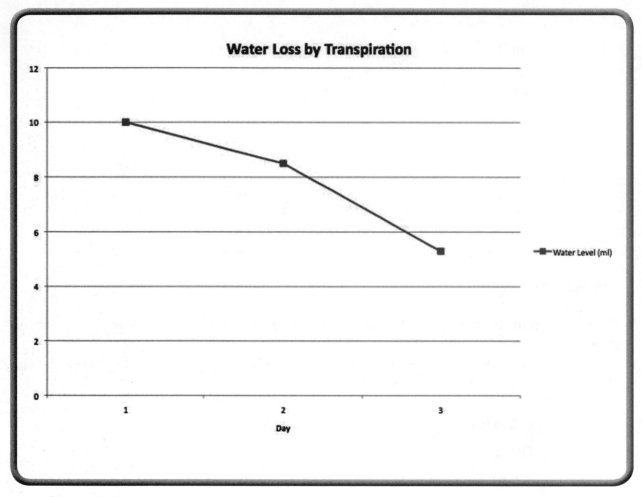

Figure 7-10

Plants Breathe!

STEM Project Overview

Students will collaborate to:

➡ Observe how environmental conditions affect a plant's ability to photosynthesize or respire. *(Science/Math)*

➡ Enter their data and display in the form of a diagram. *(Science/Technology/Engineering/Math)*

➡ Evaluate their findings. *(Science/Math)*

➡ Brainstorm to improve the experimentation process. *(Science/Engineering)*

Science

Students will understand the relationships among organisms and their physical environment, including:

• Knowing the basic needs of plants like air, water, and light

• Knowing that changes in the environment can have an effect on plants

• Using appropriate tools and simple equipment to gather scientific data and extend the senses

• Knowing that learning can come from careful observations and simple experiments

Math

Students will use mathematical analysis to pose questions, seek answers, and develop solutions, including:

• Using appropriate scientific tools to solve problems about the natural world

Engineering

Students will use engineering design to pose questions, seek answers, and develop solutions, including:

• Using a variety of verbal and graphic techniques to present conclusions

• Devising ways to determine the volume of a solid object

• Identifying simple problems and solutions

• Proposing alternative solutions for procedures

Technology

Students will know the characteristics, uses, and basic features of computer software programs, including:

• Knowing the common features and uses of desktop publishing and word processing software

• Using basic menu commands and toolbar functions

• Using advanced features of word processing

• Knowing that documents can be created, designed, and formatted

• Importing images into a document

Plants Breathe! *(cont.)*

Materials

- 4 corks or rubber stoppers to fit into test tubes (per group)
- 2 test tube racks or large beakers (per group)
- 2 Elodea plants*(two 4"–6" sections per group)
- four 25 mm x 150 ml test tubes (per group)
- aluminum foil
- 0.04% bromothymol blue solution**
- masking tape
- safety goggles (for all participants)
- sink or bucket
- straws

*An Elodea plant is a common aquatic plant sold at pet stores.
**Bromothymol blue solution is available in science supply catalogs or in high school biology labs.

Vocabulary

aquatic plant—a plant that lives in water

carbon dioxide—a colorless, odorless gas produced by respiration

control—something used in an experiment or study to provide a check on results

oxygen—a colorless, odorless gas produced by photosynthesis

photosynthesis—the process by which green plants use sunlight, water, and carbon dioxide to make food

respiration—the process by which organisms produce energy from oxygen

solution—a liquid mixture

Background

Before beginning this experiment, you should review or introduce the basic concepts of **photosynthesis** and **respiration**. The important part of the discussion should be the production of oxygen by plants when they photosynthesize and the production of carbon dioxide when we respire. In the experiment the following should occur:

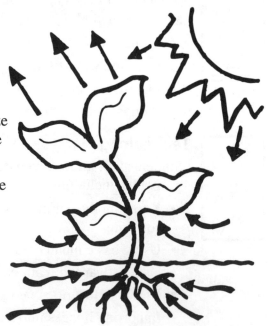

The plant exposed to sunlight in the yellow bromothymol blue solution will **photosynthesize,** which will take the carbon dioxide from the solution turning it back to blue.

The plant wrapped in foil will **respire**, which will produce carbon dioxide and turn the solution from blue to yellow.

The test tubes with no plants in them act as controls and should remain the same color.

Plants Breathe! *(cont.)*

Science Experiment Procedure

1. Make a data table similar to the one in Table 8-1. You can also make individual copies of the data table template shown on page 69.

Plants Breathe!								
Test Tube	Light	No Light	Carbon Dioxide	No Carbon Dioxide	Plant	No Plant	Start Color	End Color
A								
B								
C								
D								

Table 8-1

2. Use the masking tape to label one test tube "A," one "B," one "C," and one "D."

3. Put on the safety goggles.

4. Fill the four test tubes with water, all the way to the top.

5. Add drops of bromothymol blue solution to each test tube so the water in each tube changes to a bluish-green color.

6. Pour the water from test tubes A and B into a beaker.

7. Using a straw, gently blow bubbles into the water so it turns from bluish green to yellow. The reason the water is changing from blue to yellow is that the carbon dioxide you are blowing out from the lungs turns the bromothymol blue solution yellow. This is the carbon dioxide solution.

8. Place one 4"–6" section of an Elodea plant into test tube A.

9. Pour the yellow carbon dioxide solution into test tubes A and B, all the way to the top.

10. Discard any leftover yellow solution down the sink or in a bucket.

11. Place a cork or stopper in the top of test tubes A and B to seal them.

12. Fill out the information in the data table for test tubes A and B.

Plants Breathe! *(cont.)*

Science Experiment Procedure *(cont.)*

13. Next, add another 4"–6" section of an Elodea plant into test tube C. There are no plants in B or D.

14. Place a cork or stopper in the top of test tubes C and D to seal them. The solutions in test tubes C and D are bluish green because there is oxygen in the water and no carbon dioxide.

15. Fill out the information in the data table for test tubes C and D.

16. Completely cover test tubes C and D with aluminum foil so no light can reach the solution.

17. Place all four test tubes near a sunny window for 24 hours.

18. Take the foil off the test tubes and record the end color of the solution in each test tube.

19. Clean up per the teacher's instructions.

Brainstorming

While the class is waiting for the results of their Plants Breathe! experiment, ask them to make some predictions about what might happen to the color of the solution in each test tube.

Have a discussion about why test tubes B and D had no plants in them. This should bring up the importance of using a **control** when conducting an experiment.

Challenge the class to come up with a way to turn a yellow bromthymol blue solution back to blue. *One way is to use a small aquarium air pump and air stone to charge it with oxygen. Another way might be to place it in a closed jar and shake it until it turns blue.*

Ask the students to elaborate on why this activity is called "Plants Breathe!"

Plants Breathe! *(cont.)*

Science Experiment Procedure *(cont.)*

Plants Breathe! Data Table Templates

Plants Breathe!

Test Tube	Light	No Light	Carbon Dioxide	No Carbon Dioxide	Plant	No Plant	Start Color	End Color
A								
B								
C								
D								

Plants Breathe!

Test Tube	Light	No Light	Carbon Dioxide	No Carbon Dioxide	Plant	No Plant	Start Color	End Color
A								
B								
C								
D								

Plants Breathe! *(cont.)*

Technology Learning Objectives

At the end of this lesson, students will:

1. Change the viewing size of a document.

2. Change the page orientation of a document.

3. Use the polygon tool.

4. Copy and paste a shape.

5. Change the fill and line color of a shape.

6. Use the text box tool.

7. Change the size, color, and style of font within a text box.

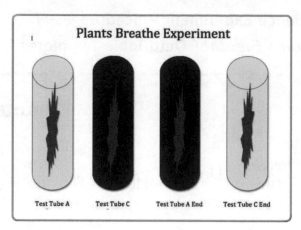

Plants Breathe Experiment

Test Tube A   Test Tube C   Test Tube A End   Test Tube C End

Figure 8-14

Teacher Note

The technology portion of this activity is written for MS Word 2010 but can be completed using most spreadsheet and word processing software versions like Open Office, Google Docs, and iWorks with minimal modification.

Technology Procedure (Part 1)

1. Open a new word processing document.

2. Go to the **View** menu and select **Zoom**. Reduce the view of the document to **75%**

3. Next, you are going to change the orientation of the document to landscape. Go to the **File** menu, select **Page Set-up**, and choose **Landscape** (Figure 8-1).

Figure 8-1

You can also go to the **Layout** menu, choose **Orientation**, and select **Landscape** (Figure 8-2).

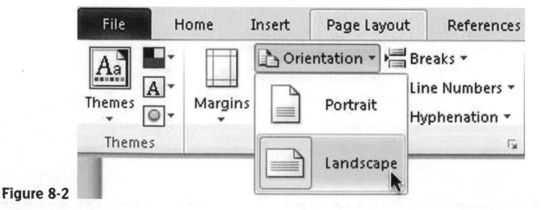

Figure 8-2

Plants Breathe! *(cont.)*

Technology Procedure (Part 1) *(cont.)*

4. Go to the **Insert** menu and select **Text Box**. Now click and drag the cursor to draw a text box along the top of the document (Figure 8-3).

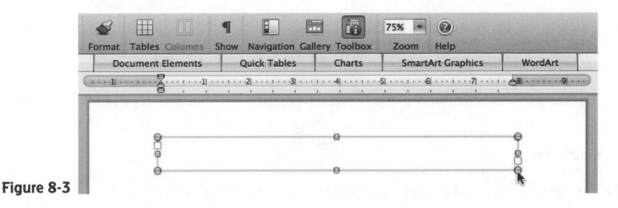

Figure 8-3

5. Click into the text box and type in the label: "Plants Breathe Experiment".

6. Click and drag over the text to highlight it.

7. Change the font size to **36** (Figure 8-4).

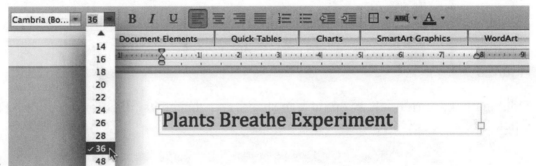

Figure 8-4

8. With the text still highlighted, use the **Align Center** button to center the text within the text box (Figure 8-5).

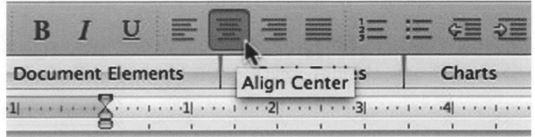

Figure 8-5

9. Next, you will use the **AutoShapes** tool. You can access AutoShapes by going to the **Insert** menu, choosing **Picture**, and then **AutoShapes**.

Plants Breathe! *(cont.)*

Technology Procedure (Part 1) *(cont.)*

10. Click on the **AutoShapes** icon, choose **Basic Shapes**, and select **Can** (Figure 8-6).

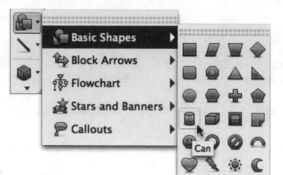

Figure 8-6

11. Use the can shape tool to draw a cylinder similar to the one in Figure 8-7.

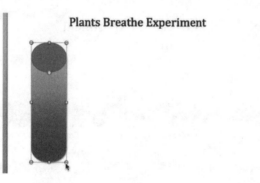

Figure 8-7

12. Double click, or right click, on the can shape, and change its fill color to yellow (Figure 8-8). Click **OK**.

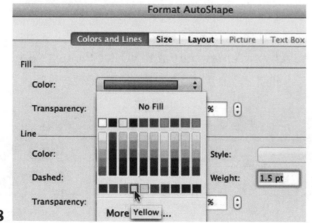

Figure 8-8

13. With the can shape still highlighted, go to the **Edit** menu and select **Copy**. You can also right click on the can and select Copy.

14. Click near the center of the page and choose **Paste** from the **Edit** menu or by right clicking on the page to bring up the **Paste** function.

Plants Breathe! *(cont.)*

Technology Procedure (Part 1) *(cont.)*

15. Now click and drag the copy of the can shape, so it is next to the first can (Figure 8-9).

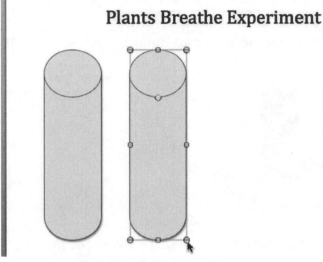

Figure 8-9

16. Paste two more cans into the document to make a total of four can shapes.

17. Now use the **Text Box** tool to draw a text box below the first can shape. Type in the following text into the text box: "Test Tube A Start."

18. Highlight the text and increase its font size to **18**. Also, use the **Align Center** button to center the text within the text box (Figure 8-10).

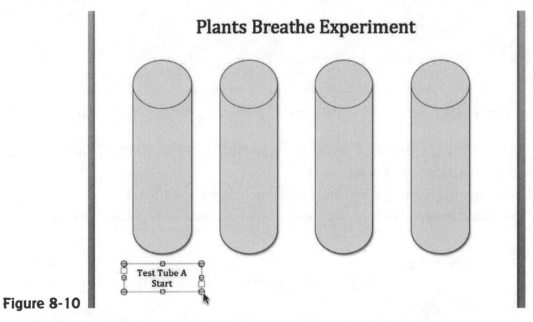

Figure 8-10

19. Repeat the same procedure to label the next shape: "Test Tube C Start."

20. Now label the third shape: "Test Tube A End," and the fourth shape: "Test Tube C End."

Plants Breathe! *(cont.)*

Technology Procedure (Part 2)

Now that the four test tubes have been created it is time to label them and add data.

1. First, change the fill color of the can shape for "Test Tube B Start" to blue.

2. Click your mouse off the page to deselect the shape.

3. Now, click on the **AutoShapes** icon, choose **Stars and Banners**, and select **Explosion 2** (Figure 8-11).

Figure 8-11

4. Use the **Shape** tool (or the **AutoShape** tool) to draw a shape within the first test tube that resembles a plant (Figure 8-12).

Test Tube A
Start

Figure 8-12

5. Double click on the plant shape and change its fill color to green.

6. Use the **Copy and Paste** function to copy the plant shape and paste it into the remaining three test tubes.

7. Finally, add the name to the document. Open the **View Menu** and choose **Header Footer**, or from the **Insert** menu choose **Header Footer**.

8. Click into the **Header** and type in a first and last name. Then click **Close** (Figure 8-13).

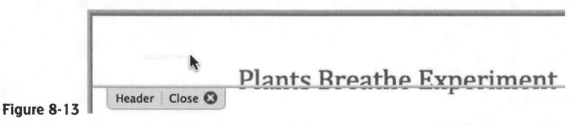

Figure 8-13

Plants Breathe! *(cont.)*

Technology Procedure (Part 2) *(cont.)*

9. Your chart is now complete. **Save** and **Print**. It should look similar to the one in Figure 8-14.

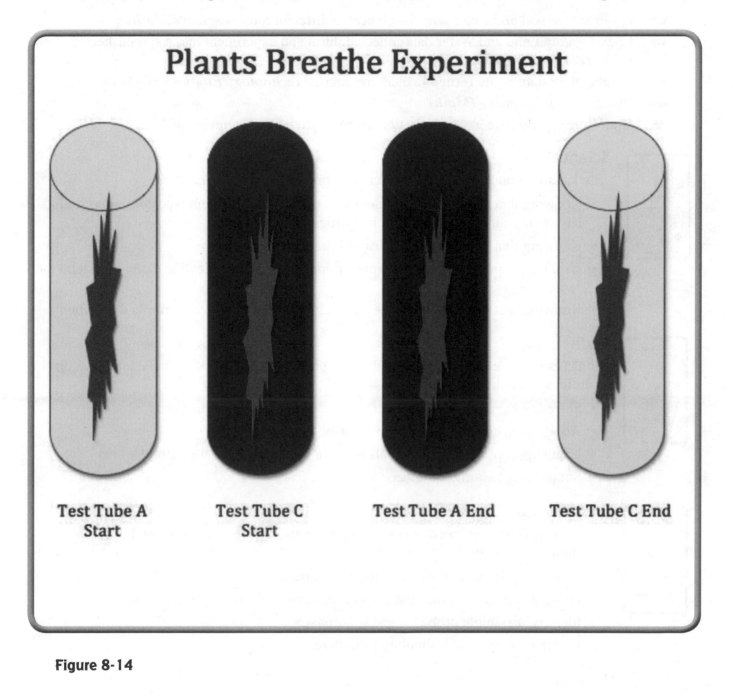

Figure 8-14

Heating Land and Water

STEM Project Overview

Students will collaborate to:

➡ Observe how soil and water will absorb heat at different rates. *(Science/Math)*

➡ Enter Heating Land and Water data collected during an experiment into a spreadsheet. *(Science/Technology/Math)*

➡ Display their data in the form of a dual line chart. *(Technology/Engineering/Math)*

➡ Evaluate their findings. *(Math)*

➡ Brainstorm to improve experimentation process. *(Science/Engineering)*

Science

Students will understand the structure and properties, including:

- Knowing that different objects are made up of many different types of materials and have many different observable properties
- Knowing that some materials absorb heat better than others
- Using appropriate tools and simple equipment to gather scientific data and extend the senses
- Knowing that learning can come from careful observations and simple experiments

Math

Students will use mathematical analysis to pose questions, seek answers, and develop solutions, including:

- Selecting the appropriate operation to solve mathematical problems
- Applying mathematical skills to describe the natural world
- Using appropriate scientific tools to solve problems about the natural world
- Subtracting two-digit numbers

Engineering

Students will use engineering design to pose questions, seek answers, and develop solutions, including:

- Proposing alternative solutions for procedures
- Using a variety of verbal and graphic techniques to present conclusions
- Identifying simple problems and solutions
- Understanding troubleshooting procedures

Technology

Students will know the characteristics, uses, and basic features of computer software programs, including:

- Knowing the common features and uses of spreadsheets
- Using spreadsheet software to update, add and delete data, and to produce charts

Heating Land and Water *(cont.)*

Materials

- two 300 or 400 ml beakers (per group)
- 2 thermometers (per group)
- dry soil or coffee grounds
- heat lamp (per group)
- ring stand (per group)
- room temperature water
- safety goggles
- stopwatch (per group)
- yardstick (per group)

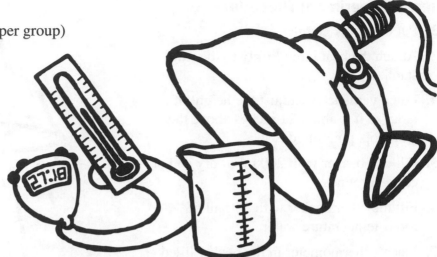

Vocabulary

absorb—to take in

reflect—to bounce off

heating—the process of increasing an object's temperature by absorbing energy

cooling—the process of lowering an object's temperature by removing energy

Background

Heat lamps work perfectly for this activity and are usually a common item that can be borrowed from a middle school or high school science lab. If a heat lamp is not available, use a 100-watt, incandescent light bulb.

Before beginning this experiment, ask the class if they think that all substances take in, or **absorb**, energy the same way. Also ask them how they could tell if an object is absorbing energy. *(Its temperature would increase.)* Then ask the class how they could tell if an object is giving off energy. *(Its temperature decreases.)*

Science Experiment Procedure

1. Make a Heating Land and Water data table similar to the one in Table 9-1 below. You can also make copies of the data table template shown on page 79.

Heating Land and Water		
Time	Temperature of Soil	Temperature of Water
0		
1		
2		
3		
4		
5		
Temperature Change Total		

Table 9-1

Heating Land and Water *(cont.)*

Science Experiment Procedure *(cont.)*

2. Put on safety goggles.

3. Attach the heat lamp firmly to the ring stand.

4. Use a yardstick to adjust the height of the lamp so it is about 21 inches above the table top, pointing down.

5. Fill one beaker with 200 ml of dry soil or coffee grounds.

6. Fill the other beaker with 200 ml of room-temperature water.

7. Place a thermometer in the beaker filled with soil so that the bulb is about halfway down in the soil. Record the temperature.

8. Place the other thermometer in the beaker containing water. Record the temperature.

9. Turn on the heat lamp and arrange the beakers so they both receive equal amounts of light.

10. Turn off the heat lamp.

11. Wait one minute and then record the temperature of both thermometers in the data table on the row for "1."

12. Turn on the heat lamp and start the stopwatch. Be careful not to touch the heart lamp because it can get very hot!

13. Record the temperature of both thermometers every minute for a total of five minutes.

14. Carefully turn off the light.

15. Finally, subtract the start temperature from the temperature at five minutes to determine the total temperature change for both thermometers and record in the data table.

Brainstorming

Once the class has completed the activity, ask students if they can think of other ways to test the ability for substances to absorb heat? What other objects could they use besides soil and water?

Ask them if they think an object's color has an effect on its ability to absorb heat.

Heating Land and Water (cont.)

Science Experiment Procedure (cont.)
Heating Land and Water Data Table Templates

Heating Land and Water		
Time ⏱	Temperature of Soil 🥛	Temperature of Water 🥛
0		
1		
2		
3		
4		
5		
Temperature Change Total		

Heating Land and Water		
Time ⏱	Temperature of Soil 🥛	Temperature of Water 🥛
0		
1		
2		
3		
4		
5		
Temperature Change Total		

Heating Land and Water *(cont.)*

Technology Learning Objectives

At the end of this lesson, students will be able to:

1. Know the various terms associated with spreadsheets including, rows, columns, and cells.

2. Enter data into a spreadsheet.

3. Adjust the width of a selected column.

4. Change the alignment of data within a cell.

5. Change the style of data within a cell.

6. Create and format a dual line chart from data entered within a spreadsheet.

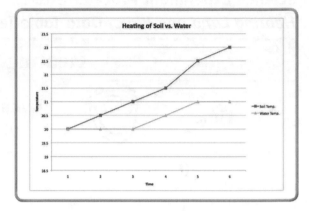

Teacher Note

The technology portion of this activity is written for MS Excel 2010 but can be completed using most spreadsheet and word processing software versions like Open Office, Google Docs, and iWorks with minimal modification.

Technology Procedure

1. Open a new spreadsheet document. Spreadsheets are made up of *columns* that are identified by letters (A, B, C, etc.) and *rows* that are identified by numbers (1, 2, 3, etc.).

2. The location within a spreadsheet where a column meets a row is called a *cell* and is identified by both a letter and number (Figure 9-1).

Figure 9-1

3. Click into cell **A1** and type in the label: "Time." Hit the **Tab** key on the keyboard to bring you over to cell **B1** and type in the label: "Soil Temp."

4. Hit the Tab key again and type in the label: "Water Temp."

5. Next, click and drag over the three column labels and use the **Bold** button on the toolbar to make the column titles bold (Figure 9-2).

Figure 9-2

6. Now fill in the data into the spreadsheet.

Heating Land and Water *(cont.)*

Technology Procedure *(cont.)*

7. Next, you will center the data in the cells. To do this, click and drag over all of the data in the spreadsheet to highlight it. Then use the **Align Center** button on the toolbar (Figure 9-3).

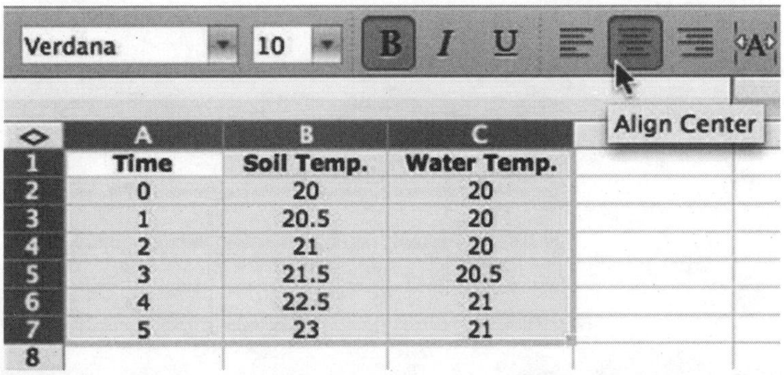

Figure 9-3

8. Now you are going to use the data to create a chart. First, highlight all of the data in both columns, including the labels. Choose the **Insert** menu, choose **Chart**, and click on **Marked Line** (Figure 9-4).

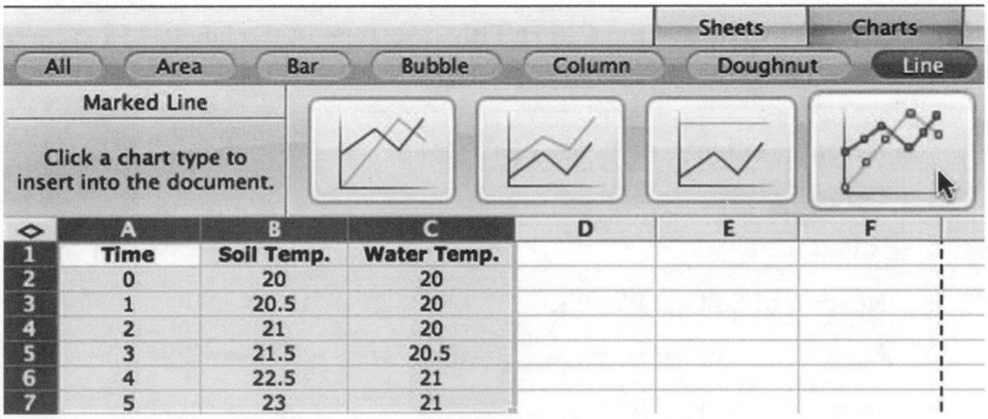

Figure 9-4

9. Your chart should now appear *within* the spreadsheet.

10. Go to the **Chart** menu, select **Move Chart**, choose **New Sheet** and click **OK** (Figure 9-5).

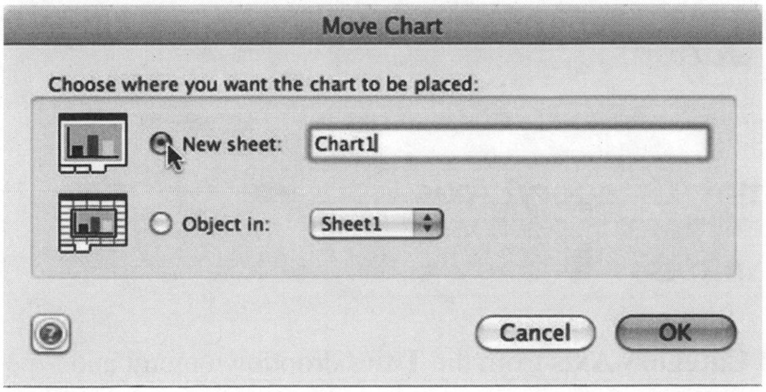

Figure 9-5

Heating Land and Water *(cont.)*

Technology Procedure *(cont.)*

11. Your chart should now take up the entire page.

12. Click on the blue line for "Time" and hit **delete** on the keyboard. This will remove the time data from the spreadsheet (Figure 9-6).

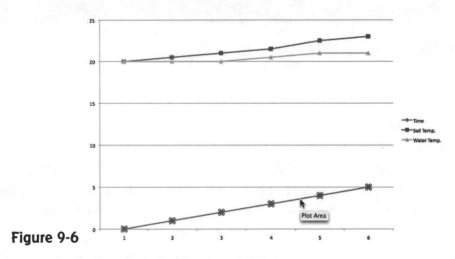

Figure 9-6

13. Next, under **Chart Options**, in the **Chart Title** box, type in the label: "Heating of Soil vs. Water" (Figure 9-7).

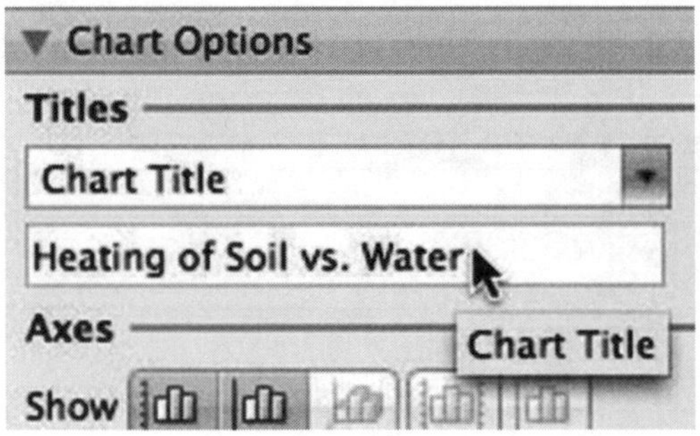

Figure 9-7

14. Under **Chart Options**, click on the **Chart Title** dropdown menu and select **Horizontal Category Axis**. Type in the following label for the horizontal axis: "Time (Minutes)" (Figure 9-8).

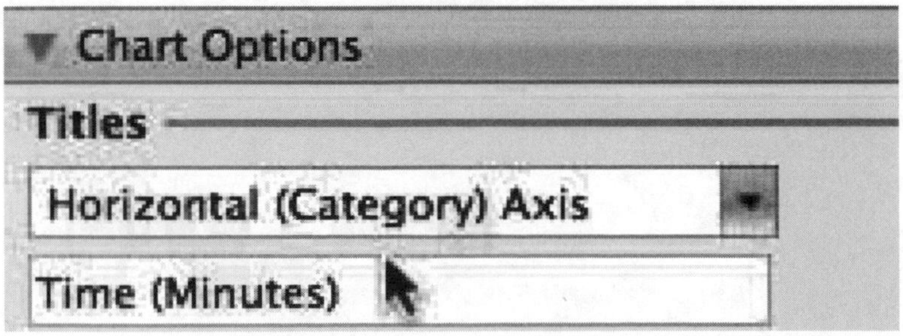

Figure 9-8

15. Next, select the **Vertical Category Axis** from the **Titles** dropdown menu and type in the label: "Temperature."

Heating Land and Water *(cont.)*

Technology Procedure *(cont.)*

16. Your chart is now complete. **Save** and **Print**. It should look similar to the one in Figure 9-9.

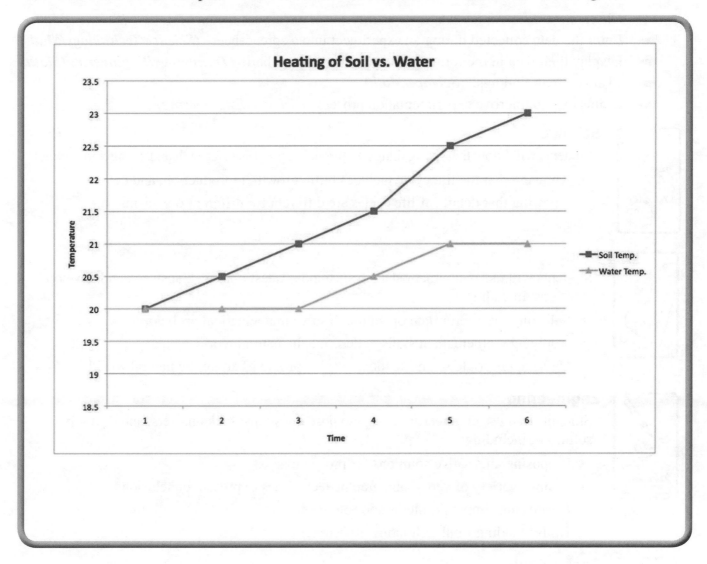

Figure 9-9

Monarch Butterfly Life Cycle

STEM Project Overview

Students will collaborate to:

➡ Observe the different life stages of an insect as it undergoes metamorphosis. **(*Science/Math*)**

➡ Enter the data collected during an experiment into a spreadsheet. **(*Science/Technology/Math*)**

➡ Display their data in the form of a diagram and a line chart. **(*Technology/Engineering/Math*)**

➡ Evaluate their findings. **(*Science/Math*)**

➡ Brainstorm to improve experimentation process. **(*Science/Engineering*)**

Science

Students will know that living things go through a process of growth and change, including:

- Knowing that the life cycle includes birth, growth, reproduction, and death
- Knowing that details of life cycles are different for different organisms

Math

Students will use mathematical analysis to pose questions, seek answers, and develop solutions, including:

- Selecting the appropriate operation to solve mathematical problems
- Applying mathematical skills to describe the natural world
- Using appropriate scientific tools to solve problems about the natural world

Engineering

Students will use engineering design to pose questions, seek answers, and develop solutions, including:

- Proposing alternative solutions for procedures
- Using a variety of verbal and graphic techniques to present conclusions
- Identifying simple problems and solutions
- Understanding troubleshooting procedures

Technology

Students will know the characteristics, uses, and basic features of computer software programs, including:

- Using the common features and uses of desktop publishing and word processing software
- Using basic menu commands and toolbar functions
- Using advanced features of word processing
- Knowing that documents can be created, designed, and formatted
- Importing images into a document
- Knowing the common features and uses of spreadsheets
- Using spreadsheet software to update, add and delete data, and to produce charts

Monarch Butterfly Life Cycle *(cont.)*

Materials

- 2-liter plastic soda bottle with top cut off (per group)
- milkweed leaves on stem (per group)
- magnifying glasses
- Monarch Butterfly eggs (1–3 eggs per group)
- paper towel
- 12" square of netting or cheesecloth (per group)
- rubber band
- ruler (metric)

Vocabulary

egg—round object laid by an animal to reproduce, from which young hatch

larva—the wingless form of an insect that hatches from an egg

caterpillar—wormlike larva of an insect

chrysalis—a moth or butterfly that is encased in a firm protective case

frass—waste produced by larva

adult—fully developed form of an animal

Background

There are many websites that can be used as good resources for learning how to best raise Monarchs in the classroom.

Before beginning this experiment, you will have to obtain Monarch butterfly eggs and a source for milkweed leaves. Both can be obtained online, at low cost. Or, if a field exists nearby that has common milkweed plants growing, you may also find eggs on the undersides of the leaves.

The milkweed leaves will be used for food for the caterpillars as they grow. Milkweed plants can be harvested and the stems of the plants kept in water to keep them fresh. You can also store milkweed leaves in a plastic bag in a refrigerator to keep them fresh. It is important to have an ample supply of fresh milkweed for the caterpillars to use as food.

Science Experiment Procedure

1. Use a magnifying glass to observe the eggs. Measure the length of the Monarch egg using a metric ruler.

2. Record the length of the egg in the Monarch Life Cycle data table like the one shown in Table 10-1. See page 87 for data table templates.

Monarch Life Cycle	
Life Cycle Stage	**Length (cm)**
Egg	

Table 10-1

Monarch Butterfly Life Cycle *(cont.)*

Science Experiment Procedure *(cont.)*

3. Place a section of milkweed plant with the egg on it in the plastic container. Make sure that you wrap the base of the stem of the milkweed plant with a damp paper towel to help keep it fresh.

4. Cover the container with a piece of netting or cheesecloth and secure it with a rubber band.

5. Put the container in a warm location (at least 68 degrees F) and observe it every day.

6. Your egg should hatch in 3–5 days. Once the caterpillar emerges from the egg, use the ruler to estimate its length. Please do not touch the caterpillar when you measure it. Record the life stage and length of the caterpillar in the data table.

7. Your caterpillar will be eating the milkweed leaves as food. Make sure that it has a fresh supply of milkweed.

8. As the caterpillar grows, continue to estimate its length, and record it in the data table. The caterpillar will be eating a lot of milkweed as it grows. As a result, it produces waste in the form of small green pellets. These pellets are called *frass* and they will collect at the bottom of the container. Every few days the frass needs to be cleaned out. Carefully remove the milkweed with the caterpillar to clean the habitat (plastic container) and then replace them gently.

9. Your caterpillars will grow rapidly over a two-week period. They will shed their skin five times to accommodate their growing size.

10 After approximately 10–14 days, the caterpillar will attach itself under a leaf or at the top of the container and make a "J" shape. It will then form a hardened outer covering called a chrysalis. The insect is now in the pupa stage. Record the length of the chrysalis in the data table.

11 The pupa will appear green for about 9–14 days. When it begins to turn black, the butterfly will soon emerge.

12. Estimate the length of the butterfly and record it in the data table. After about one hour, the butterfly will be ready to fly away!

Brainstorming

Once the class has completed the activity, ask students if they can think of any ways that they could improve their experiment by coming up with safe ways of determining the mass of the different stages of butterfly development.

Challenge the class to design better butterfly habitats.

Monarch Butterfly Life Cycle (cont.)

Science Experiment Procedure (cont.)
Monarch Life Cycle Data Table Templates

Monarch Butterfly Life Cycle	
Life Cycle Stage	Length (cm)
Egg	

Monarch Butterfly Life Cycle	
Life Cycle Stage	Length (cm)
Egg	

Monarch Butterfly Life Cycle *(cont.)*

Technology Learning Objectives – Procedures A and B

At the end of this lesson, students will:

1. Know the various terms associated with spreadsheets including rows, columns, and cells.
2. Enter data into a spreadsheet.
3. Adjust the width of a selected column.
4. Change the alignment and style of data within a cell.
5. Create and format a line chart from data entered within a spreadsheet
6. Change the page layout for a word processing document.
7. Insert WordArt into a document.
8. Use the Block Arrows tool.
9. Insert an image into a word processing document.
10. Use the Text Box tool to create labels.

Growth Rate of a Monarch Butterfly

Figure 10-20

Teacher Notes

This activity is divided into two parts. The first part has the students use their butterfly length data to make a line chart using spreadsheet software. The second part has students using word processing to create a diagram of a butterfly's life cycle. The two parts should be done on separate days.

The technology portion of this activity is written for MS Excel and Word 2010 but can be completed using most spreadsheet and word processing software versions like Open Office, Google Docs, and iWorks with minimal modification.

Images used in this activity are courtesy of *joyfulbutterfly.com*, which is a website that provides free butterfly images that can be inserted into student projects.

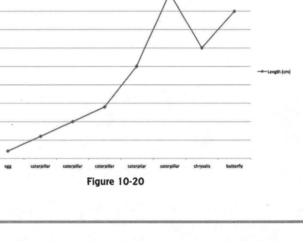

Technology Procedure A

1. Open a new word processing document.
2. Go to the **View** menu and select **Zoom**. Reduce the view of the document to **75%**, then hit OK.
3. Next, change the orientation of the document to landscape. Go to the **File** menu, select **Page Set-up**, and choose **Landscape** (Figure 10-1) and hit **OK**.

Figure 10-1

Monarch Butterfly Life Cycle *(cont.)*

Technology Procedure A *(cont.)*

You can also go to the **Layout** menu, choose **Orientation**, and select **Landscape** (Figure 10-2).

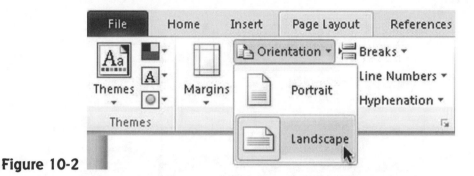

Figure 10-2

4. Go to the **Insert** menu and select a **WordArt** style, then click on it to insert it into the document (Figure 10-3).

Figure 10-3

5. Click and drag the **WordArt** box to the top and center of the document.

6. Double click on the **WordArt** text to bring up the **Edit WordArt Text** box. Now type in the following title: "Monarch Butterfly Life Cycle."

7. Click **OK** and drag the text so it is centered at the top of the page.

8. Next, you will use the **AutoShapes** tool. Access **AutoShapes** by going to the **Insert** menu. Choose **Picture** and **AutoShapes**.

9. Click on the **AutoShapes** (or **Shapes**) icon, choose **Block Arrows**, and select **Right Arrow Callout** (Figure10-4).

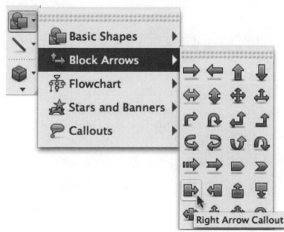

Figure 10-4

Monarch Butterfly Life Cycle *(cont.)*

Technology Procedure A *(cont.)*

10. Click and drag the cursor directly underneath the title of the document to draw the first callout box similar to the one in Figure 10-5.

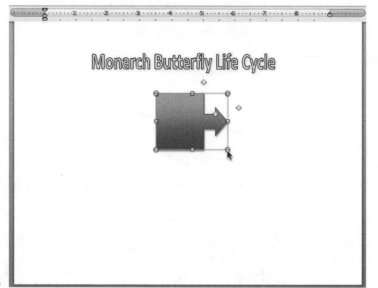

Figure 10-5

11. Open up the web browser and go to the following website: *www.joyfulbutterfly.com.*

12. Click on the **Free Photos** link.

13. On the free photos page, click on the **Free Butterfly Egg Photos**. Find a good picture of a Monarch butterfly egg and click on it.

14. Right click on the image and choose **Copy Image**. You can also go to the **Edit** menu, choose **Select All**, then **Copy**.

15. Go back to the word processing document, choose the **Edit** menu and select **Paste** to insert the image of the butterfly egg into the document.

16. Click on one of the anchor points on the corner of the image and drag it so the picture is the same size as the arrow callout box (Figure 10-6).

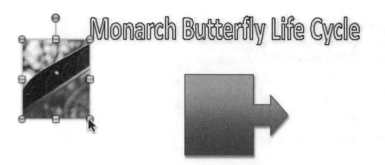

Figure 10-6

Monarch Butterfly Life Cycle *(cont.)*

Technology Procedure A *(cont.)*

17. Next, right click on the image of the butterfly egg, select **Arrange**, and choose **In Front of Text** (Figure 10-7). Or double click on the image, choose **Layout**, and select **In Front of Text**. Click **OK**.

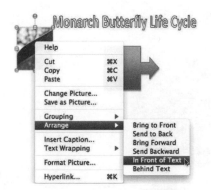

Figure 10-7

18. Click and drag the image so it fits within the arrow box (Figure 10-8).

Figure 10-8

19. Click on the **AutoShapes** icon, choose **Block Arrows**, and this time select **Down Arrow Callout**. Use it to draw a shape similar to the one in Figure 10-9.

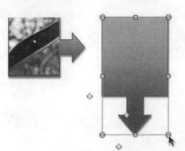

Figure 10-9

20. Copy and paste an image of a Monarch caterpillar from the Internet and resize it so it fits in the callout box. Make sure to right click on the image of the caterpillar, select **Arrange**, and choose **In Front of Text.**

Monarch Butterfly Life Cycle (cont.)

Technology Procedure A (cont.)

21. Next, click on the **AutoShapes** icon, choose **Block Arrows**, and this time select **Left Arrow Callout**. Use it to draw a shape similar to the one in Figure 10-10.

Figure 10-10

22. Copy and paste an image of a Monarch chrysalis from the internet and resize it so it fits in the callout box. Make sure to right click on the image of the chrysalis, select **Arrange**, and choose **In Front of Text**.

23. Next, click on the **AutoShapes** icon, choose **Block Arrows**, and this time select **Up Arrow Callout**. Use it to draw a shape similar to the one in Figure 10-11.

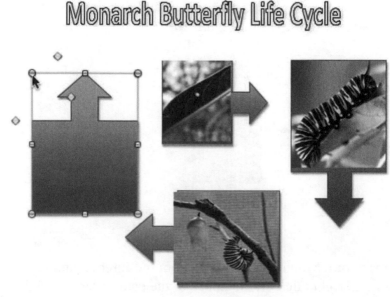

Figure 10-11

Monarch Butterfly Life Cycle (cont.)

Technology Procedure A (cont.)

24. Copy and paste an image of a Monarch butterfly from the Internet and resize it so it fits in the callout box. Make sure to right click on the image of the butterfly, select **Arrange**, and choose **In Front of Text**.

25. Your chart is now complete. **Save** and **Print**. It should appear like the one in Figure 10-12.

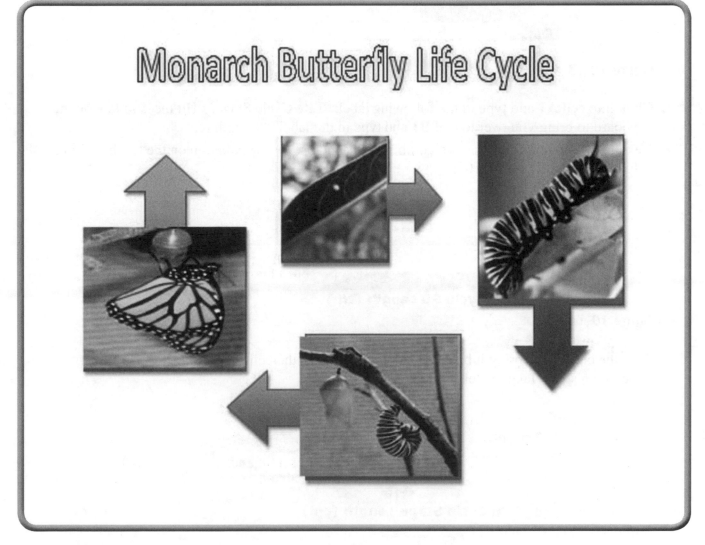

Figure 10-12

Monarch Butterfly Life Cycle *(cont.)*

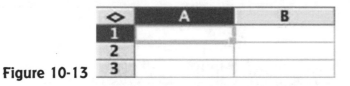

Technology Procedure B

1. Open a new spreadsheet document. Spreadsheets are made up of *columns* that are identified by letters (A, B, C, etc.) and *rows* that are identified by numbers (1, 2, 3, etc.).

2. The location within a spreadsheet where a column meets a row is called a *cell* and is identified by both a letter and number (Figure 10-13).

◇	A	B
1		
2		
3		

Figure 10-13

3. Click into cell **A1** and type in the following label: "Life Cycle Stage." Hit the **Tab** key on the keyboard to bring you over to cell **B1** and type in the label: "Length (cm)."

4. Next, click and drag over the two column labels and use the **Bold** button on the toolbar to make the column titles bold (Figure 10-14).

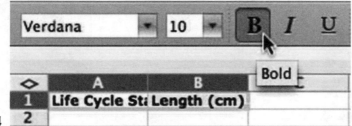

Figure 10-14

5. Take the cursor and bring it between columns A and B, then click and drag it to the right to widen the column so the label in cell **B1** fits (Figure 10-15).

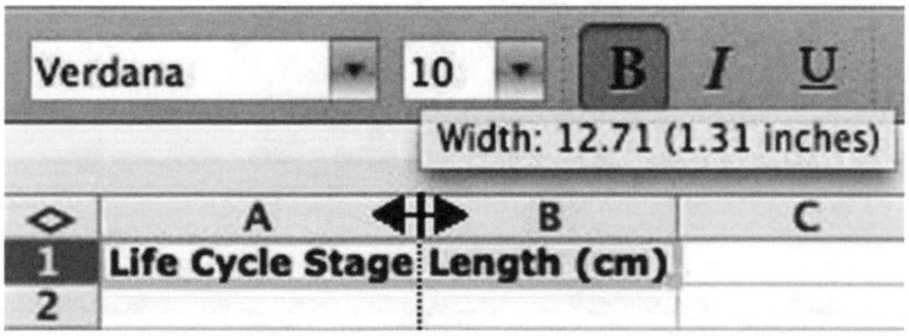

Figure 10-15

6. Now fill in the data on the growth of the Monarch into the spreadsheet.

Monarch Butterfly Life Cycle *(cont.)*

Technology Procedure B *(cont.)*

7. Next, you will center the data in the cells. To do this, click and drag over all of the data in the spreadsheet to highlight it. Then use the **Align Center** button on the toolbar (Figure 10-16).

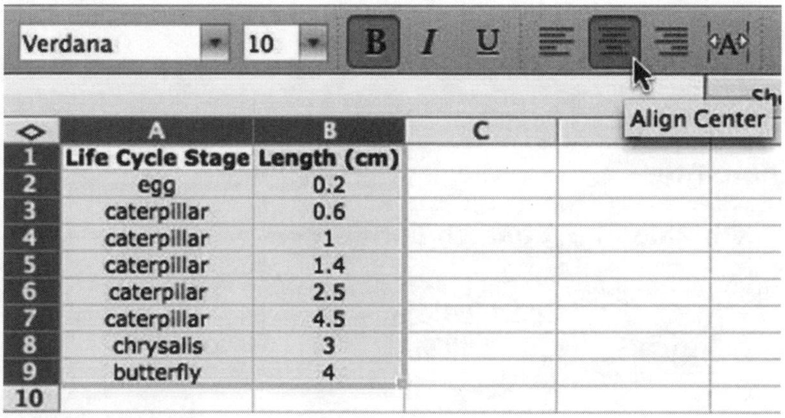

Figure 10-16

8. Now you are going to use the data to create a chart. First, highlight all of the data in both columns, including the labels. Choose the **Insert** menu, choose **Chart**, and click on **Marked Line Chart** (Figure 10-17).

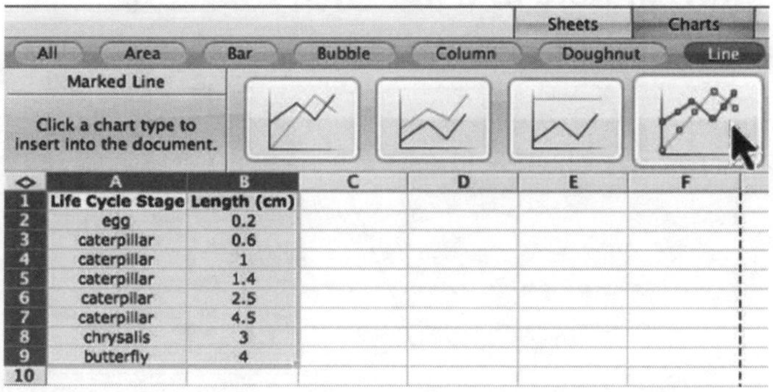

Figure 10-17

9. Your chart should now appear within the spreadsheet.

10. Go to the **Chart** menu, select **Move Chart**, choose **New Sheet** and click **OK** (Figure 10-18).

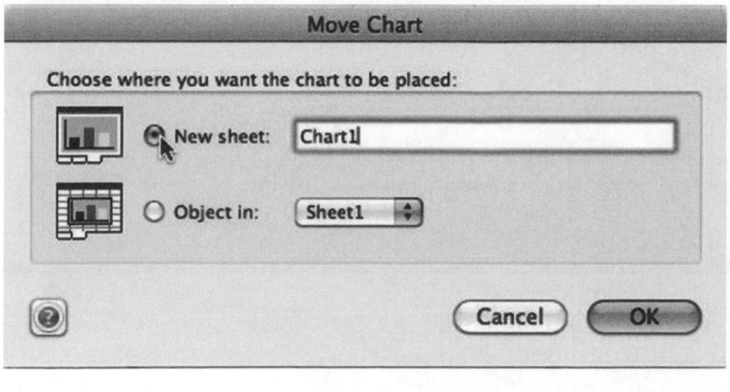

Figure 10-18

Monarch Butterfly Life Cycle *(cont.)*

Technology Procedure B *(cont.)*

11. Your chart should now take up the entire page.

12. Next, under **Chart Options**, in the **Chart Title** box, type in the title: **Growth Rate of a Monarch Butterfly** (Figure 10-19).

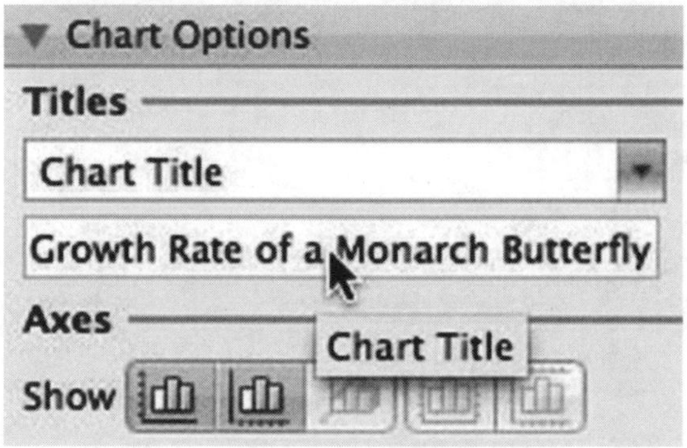

Figure 10-19

13. Your chart is now complete. **Save** and **Print**. It should look similar to the one in Figure 10-20.

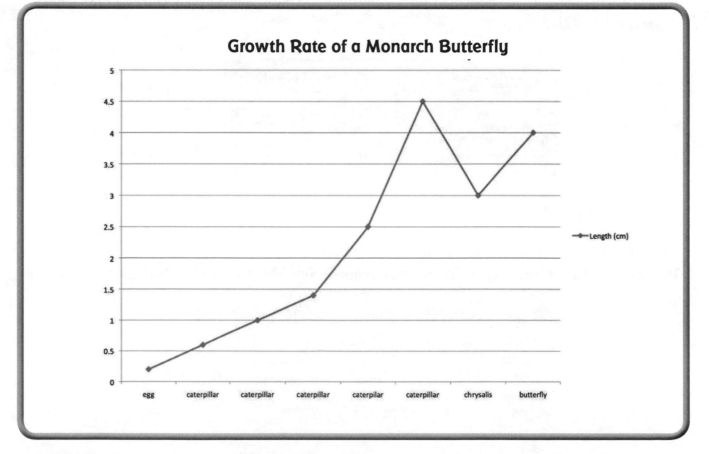

Figure 10-20

Weather Observations

Stem Project Overview

Students will collaborate to:

- Observe three daily characteristics of weather. ***(Science/Math)***

- Enter the characteristics of the Earth's Atmosphere data collected from making observations. ***(Technology/Math)***

- Display their data in the form of a line chart. ***(Technology/Engineering/Math)***

- Evaluate findings. ***(Science/Math)***

- Use the internet to gather information. ***(Technology)***

- Brainstorm to improve experimentation process. ***(Science and Engineering)***

Science Standards

Students will understand atmospheric processes, including:

- Knowing that weather conditions describe how sunny, cloudy, warm, cool, wet, or dry it is outside

Math Standards

Students will use mathematical analysis to pose questions, seek answers, and develop solutions, including:

- Selecting the appropriate operation to solve mathematical problems
- Applying mathematical skills to describe the natural world
- Using appropriate scientific tools to solve problems about the natural world
- Subtracting two digit numbers

Engineering Standards

Students will use engineering design, to pose questions, seek answers, and develop solutions, including:

- Proposing alternative solutions for procedures
- Using a variety of verbal and graphic techniques to present conclusions
- Identifying simple problems and solutions

Technology Standards

Students will know the characteristics, uses, and basic features of computer software programs, including:

- Knowing the common features and uses of spreadsheets.
- Using spreadsheet software to update, add, and delete data and to produce charts

Weather Observations

Materials

- thermometer (per group)
- stopwatch (per group)
- computer with Internet access
- *Weather Observations* Data Table Template (page 99)
- barometer (optional)

Vocabulary

air pressure—the weight of the air
air—the colorless, odorless gas that makes up the atmosphere
atmosphere—the gas that surrounds the earth
barometer—an instrument used to measure air pressure
millibar—unit of measure (mb) used to measure atmospheric pressure
thermometer—an instrument used to measure temperature

Background

Have a discussion with the class about the job a meteorologist does. After students have shared their ideas, confirm that meteorologists observe the weather by measuring different characteristics of the Earth's atmosphere. Three common measurements include *temperature, atmospheric pressure,* and *cloud cover.* This information is useful for forecasting the weather.

Later, find a spot outside of the school where the students will be able to safely measure the air temperature each day for five days. Choose a location where students will be able to see as much of the sky as possible to observe cloud cover.

Students will access the National Weather Service website *(www.weather.gov)* to get the latest air pressure measurement for your location. Post the school ZIP code near the computer. Also, make sure to instruct students to record the air pressure in millibars (mb).

Science Experiment Procedure

1. Determine who in the group will hold the thermometer, who will time the activity using the stopwatch, and who will record the data. Rotate these tasks each day.

2. Begin by using the thermometer to measure the temperature of the air outside of your classroom. Pick a spot out of direct sunlight and stand still, holding the thermometer.

3. Hold the thermometer carefully while being timed for two minutes and then take a reading.

4. Record temperature for Day 1 on a data table similar to the one in table 11-1. You can also make copies of the *Characteristics of the Earth's Atmosphere* data table template on page 100.

Characteristics of the Earth's Atmosphere					
Day	1	2	3	4	5
Temperature					
Air Pressure					
Sky Cover					

Table 11-1

Weather Observations *(cont.)*

Science Experiment Procedure *(cont.)*

5. Next, observe the sky and record it as being one of the following sky conditions:

   Clear (no clouds)

   Cloudy (all clouds and no blue sky)

   Partly Cloudy (some clouds and some blue sky)

6. Now go inside and access a computer. Navigate to the following website: *http://www.weather.gov.*

7. In the upper left-hand corner of the webpage, type in the ZIP code that your teacher instructed you to use. Click the **Go** button.

8. A forecast for your town will appear. Scroll down until you see the **Current Conditions** box on the right side of the page. Look for the **Barometer** reading and record it in the space reserved for **Air Pressure**. Double check with the classroom barometer if one is available.

9. Repeat the above procedures for the next four days.

Brainstorming

Challenge the class to come up with a design for a device they can use to hold their thermometer safely outside for the four-day period. It should be able to hold the thermometer up in the air, protect it from winds, and keep it out of direct sunlight.

Also, once they have completed their spreadsheet and chart, ask the students to identify the relationship between pressure and temperature. Once they have correctly identified that the two are indirectly related *(as pressure increases, temperature decreases)* ask them how this information may help meteorologists predict the weather.

Math Crunch

Once the four days of data gathering are complete, have students use their data to fill in the Math Crunch Chart below or the Math Crunch Chart on page 100 and determine the temperature change between each day using subtraction. If appropriate, students can continue adding information after day 4.

Temperature Day 1	Temperature Day 2	Temperature Change
Temperature Day 2	**Temperature Day 3**	**Temperature Change**
Temperature Day 3	**Temperature Day 4**	**Temperature Change**

Weather Observations *(cont.)*

Science Experiment Procedure *(cont.)*

Characteristics of the Earth's Atmosphere Data Table Template

Characteristics of the Earth's Atmosphere					
Day	**1**	**2**	**3**	**4**	**5**
Temperature					
Air Pressure					
Sky Cover					

Math Crunch Template

Math Crunch Chart		
Temperature Day 1	**Temperature Day 2**	**Temperature Change**
Temperature Day 2	**Temperature Day 3**	**Temperature Change**
Temperature Day 3	**Temperature Day 4**	**Temperature Change**
Temperature Day 4	**Temperature Day 5**	**Temperature Change**
Temperature Day 5	**Temperature Day 6**	**Temperature Change**

Weather Observations *(cont.)*

Technology Learning Objectives

At the end of this lesson, students will:

1. Know the various terms associated with spreadsheets including, rows, columns, and cells.

2. Enter data into a spreadsheet.

3. Adjust the width of a selected column.

4. Change the alignment of data within a cell.

5. Change the style of data within a cell.

6. Create and format a dual line chart from data entered within a spreadsheet.

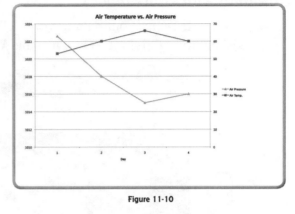

Figure 11-10

Teacher Note

The technology portion of this activity is written for MS Excel 2010 but can be completed using most spreadsheet and word processing software versions like Open Office, Google Docs, and iWorks with minimal modification.

Technology Procedure

1. Open a new spreadsheet document. Spreadsheets are made up of *columns* that are identified by letters (A, B, C, etc.) and *rows* that are identified by numbers (1, 2, 3, etc.).

2. The location within a spreadsheet where a column meets a row is called a *cell* and is identified by both a letter and number (Figure 11-1).

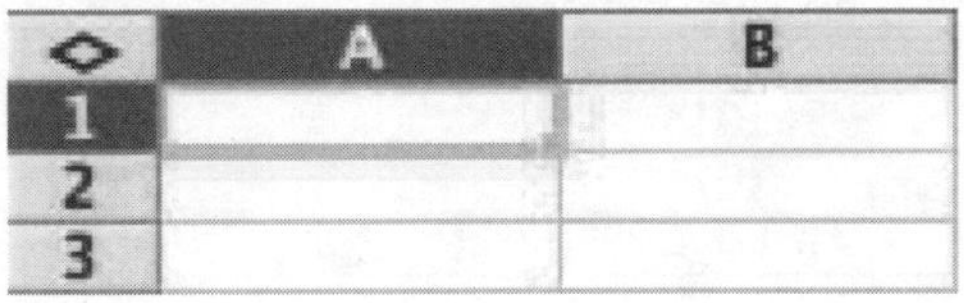

Figure 11-1

3. Click into cell **A1** and type in the following label, "Day." Hit the **Tab** key on your keyboard to bring you over to cell **B1** and type in the label "Air Temperature."

4. Hit the **Tab** key again and type in the following label: "Air Pressure."

5. Next, click and drag over the three column labels and use the **Bold** button on your toolbar to make your column titles bold (Figure 11-2).

Figure 11-2

6. Now fill in your data into your spreadsheet.

Weather Observations *(cont.)*

Technology Procedure *(cont.)*

7. Next, you will center your data in your cells. To do this, click and drag over all of the data in your spreadsheet to highlight it. Then use the **Align Center** button on your toolbar (Figure 11-3).

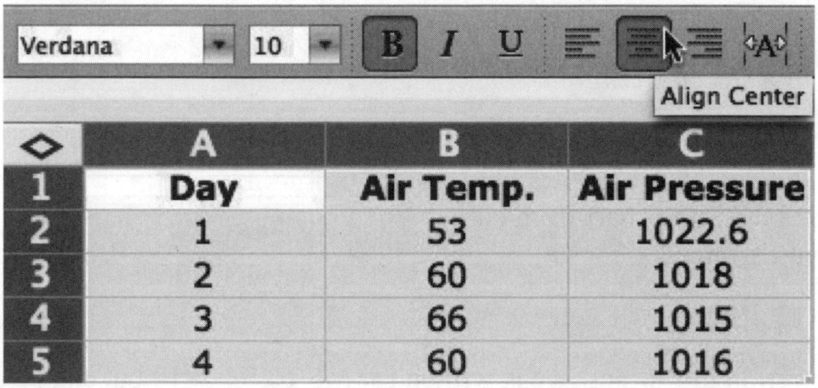

	A	B	C
1	**Day**	**Air Temp.**	**Air Pressure**
2	1	53	1022.6
3	2	60	1018
4	3	66	1015
5	4	60	1016

Figure 11-3

8. Now you are going to use your data to create a chart. First, highlight all of your data in both columns, including the labels. Choose the **Insert** menu, choose **Chart**, and click on **Marked Line Chart** (Figure 11-4).

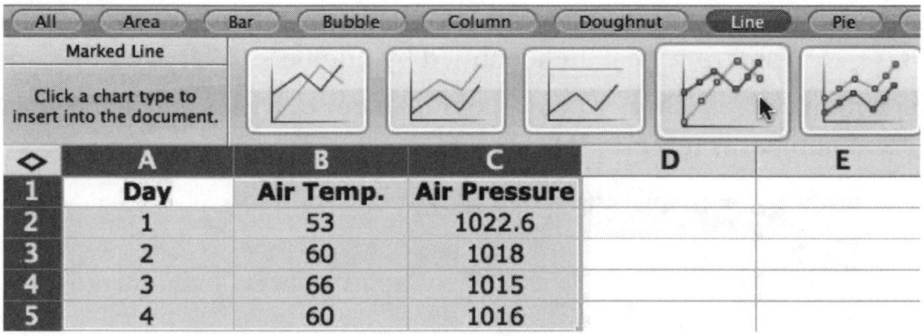

	A	B	C	D	E
1	**Day**	**Air Temp.**	**Air Pressure**		
2	1	53	1022.6		
3	2	60	1018		
4	3	66	1015		
5	4	60	1016		

Figure 11-4

9. Your chart should now appear within your spreadsheet.

10. Go to the **Chart** menu, select **Move Chart**, choose **New Sheet,** and click **OK** (Figure 11-5).

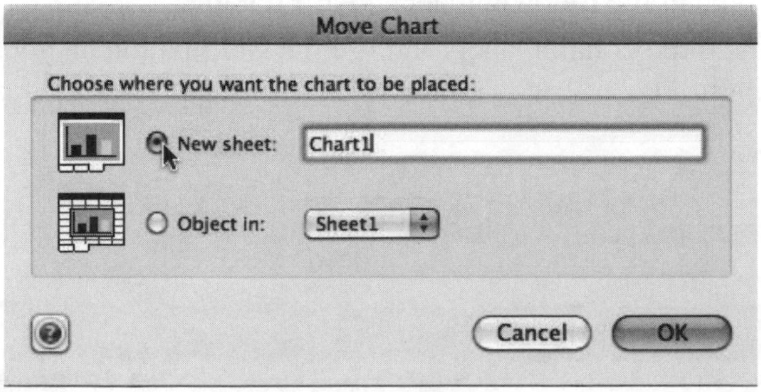

Figure 11-5

11. Your chart should now take up the entire page.

Weather Observations *(cont.)*

Technology Procedure *(cont.)*

12. Right click (Control click on a Mac) on the blue line for **Day** and hit **Delete** on your keyboard. This will remove the day data from your spreadsheet (Figure 11-6).

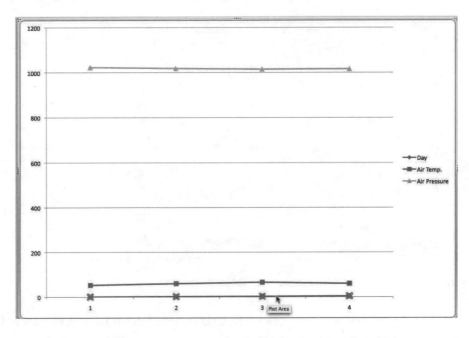

Figure 11-6

13. Next, under **Chart Options**, in the **Chart Title** box, type in the title: "Air Temperature vs. Air Pressure" (Figure 11-7).

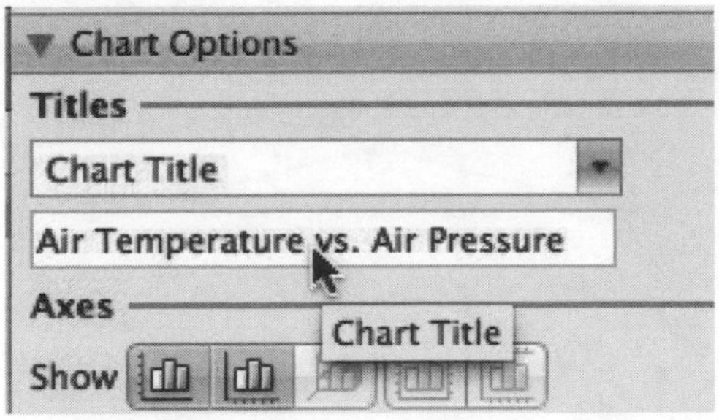

Figure 11-7

14. Under **Chart Options**, click on the **Chart Title** dropdown menu and select **Horizontal Category Axis**. Type in the following label for the horizontal axis: "Day" (Figure 11-8).

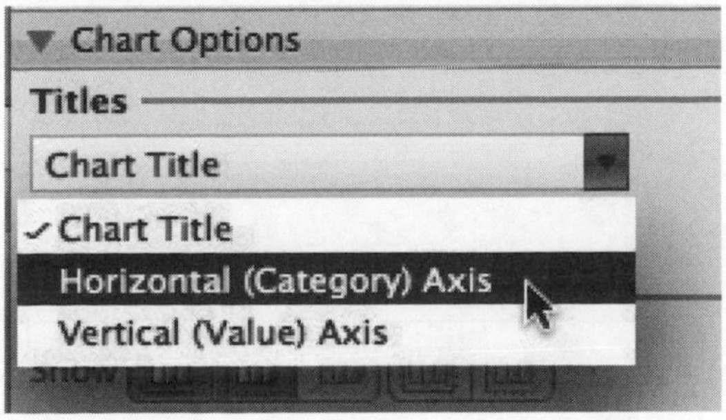

Figure 11-8

Weather Observations *(cont.)*

Technology Procedure *(cont.)*

15. Next, double click on one of the data points on the line for "Air Temperature," to bring up the **Format Data Series** window (Figure 11-9).

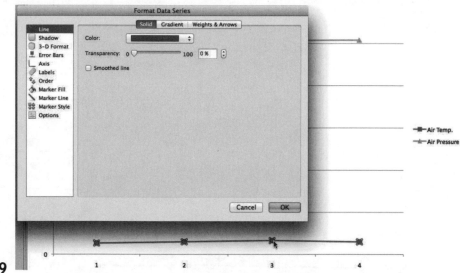

Figure 11-9

16. In the **Format Data Series** window, click on **Axis**, select **Secondary Axis**, and click **OK**.

17. Your chart is now complete and should look similar to the one in Figure 11-10.

18. **Save** and **Print** the Air Temperature vs. Air Pressure chart.

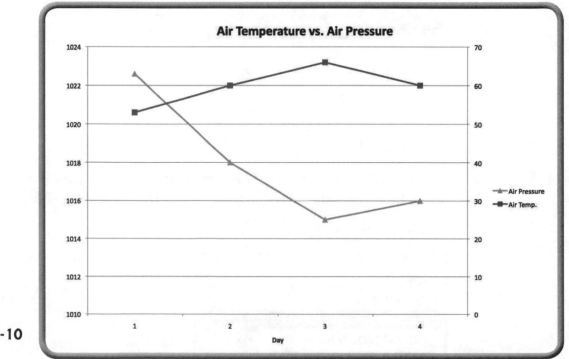

Figure 11-10

Pressure Bounce!

Stem Project Overview

Students will collaborate to:

➡ Observe how air pressure affects how high a ball will bounce. *(Science/Math)*

➡ Enter Pressure data collected from making observations. *(Science/Technology/Math)*

➡ Display their data in the form of a line chart. *(Technology/Engineering/Math)*

➡ Evaluate their findings about air pressure. *(Science/Math)*

➡ Use the internet to gather information. *(Technology)*

➡ Brainstorming to improve experimentation process. *(Science/Engineering)*

Science

Students will understand the structure and properties of matter, including:

- Knowing that things can be done to materials to change their properties

Math

Students will use mathematical analysis to pose questions, seek answers, and develop solutions, including:

- Selecting the appropriate operation to solve mathematical problems
- Applying mathematical skills to describe the natural world
- Using appropriate scientific tools to solve problems about the natural world
- Adding whole numbers

Engineering

Students will use engineering design to pose questions, seek answers, and develop solutions, including:

- Proposing alternative solutions for procedures
- Using a variety of verbal and graphic techniques to present conclusions
- Identifying simple problems and solutions

Technology

Students will know the characteristics, uses, and basic features of computer software programs, including:

- Knowing the common features and uses of spreadsheets
- Using spreadsheet software to update, add and delete data, and to produce charts

Pressure Bounce! *(cont.)*

Materials

- ball inflation needle
- ball inflation pressure gauge
- ball inflation pump
- inflatable balls—*basketball, kickball,* or *playground ball* (one per group)
- yard stick and tape measure (per group)

Vocabulary

air pressure—the force of air pressing on a surface, or the weight of the air

pressure—the force applied to a surface

psi—a unit of measurement that stands for pound-force per square inch

Background

Find out the recommended maximum air pressure required for the type(s) of ball(s) you are using. It is usually printed near the inflation point on the ball. Make sure the ball you are using is inflated to its maximum pressure before beginning this activity. This activity can be done as a whole class, or if you have more than one ball, you can break the class up into small groups. Ideally, each group will have three students, one to hold and bounce the ball, one to measure the bounce, and one to record the psi and the height. Allow students to test each ball more than once.

Prepare a table to record the **Pressure (psi)** of the ball being tested and the **Height (inches)** it will bounce. Make a table for each ball being tested three ways. (See page 107, Table 12-1.)

Science Experiment Procedure

Take turns bouncing the ball to get a feel for how high it will bounce. Do some practice measuring.

Round 1

1. Use the ball pressure gauge to determine the pressure of the fully inflated ball. Record pressure for the fully inflated ball in your *Pressure* Data Table.
2. One student should hold a yardstick with the zero end on the floor and prepare to mark the height of the ball's bounce.
3. Have another student hold the ball as high as he or she can over the floor and then drop it.
4. Observe how high the ball bounces off the floor using the yardstick. If the ball bounces higher than the yardstick, use a measuring tape to estimate the height of the bounce.
5. Record the height in your data table.

Round 2

1. Use the inflation pin to reduce the ball pressure by half.
2. Record the new pressure in your data table.
3. Drop the half-inflated ball and record its bounce height.

Round 3

1. Use the inflation needle to completely deflate the ball so the inside pressure is zero.
2. Drop the ball and record its bounce height.

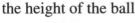

Brainstorming

What other ways might the height of the ball's bounce be measured?

Pressure Bounce! *(cont.)*

Science Experiment Procedure *(cont.)*

Pressure Data Table Template

		Pressure (psi)	Height (inches)
Fully Inflated Ball			
Inflated Ball			
Deflated Ball			

Table 12-1

Math Crunch

1. Use the *Pressure* data to fill in the table below.
2. Determine the change in pressure for each part of the experiment using subtraction.

Math Crunch Chart		
Pressure for the fully inflated ball	**Pressure for the partially inflated ball**	**Pressure Change**
Pressure for the partially inflated ball	**Pressure for the deflated ball**	**Pressure Change**
Pressure for the fully inflated ball	**Pressure for the deflated ball**	**Pressure Change**

Pressure Bounce! *(cont.)*

Technology Learning Objectives

At the end of this lesson, students will:

1. Know the various terms associated with spreadsheets, including rows, columns, and cells.

2. Enter data into a spreadsheet.

3. Adjust the width of a selected column.

4. Change the alignment of data within a cell.

5. Change the style of data within a cell.

6. Create and format a dual line chart from data entered within a spreadsheet.

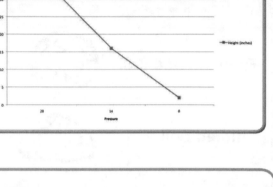

Teacher Note

The technology portion of this activity is written for MS Excel 2010 but can be completed using most spreadsheet and word processing software versions like Open Office, Google Docs, and iWorks with minimal modification.

Technology Procedure

1. Open a new spreadsheet document. Spreadsheets are made up of *columns* that are identified by letters (A, B, C, etc.) and *rows* that are identified by numbers (1, 2, 3, etc.).

2. The location within a spreadsheet where a column meets a row is called a *cell* and is identified by both a letter and number (Figure 12-1).

Figure 12-1

3. Click into cell **A1** and type in the following label: "Pressure (psi)". Hit the **Tab** key on your keyboard to bring you over to cell **B1** and type in the label: "Height (inches)."

4. Next, click and drag over the three column labels and use the **Bold** button on your toolbar to make your column titles bold (Figure 12-2).

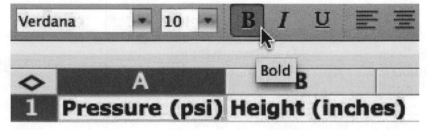

Figure 12-2

Pressure Bounce! *(cont.)*

Technology Procedure *(cont.)*

5. Widen the columns in your spreadsheet so the labels fit into the cells. To do this, click in between columns A and B and drag to the right to widen column A (Figure 12-3).

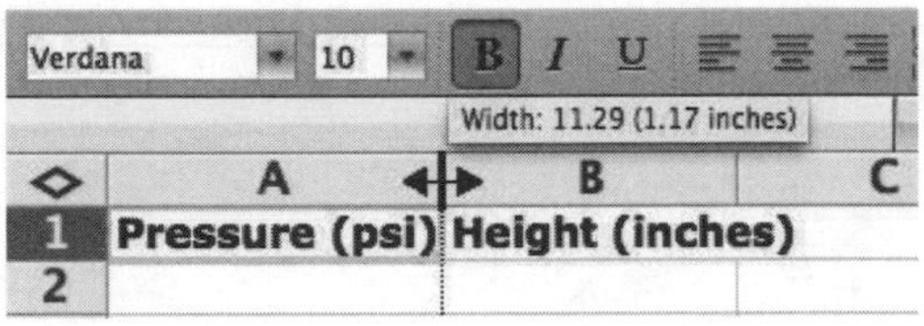

Figure 12-3

6. Repeat the same procedure for widening column B by placing the cursor between B and C and dragging it to the right.

7. Enter the data from your *Pressure* data table into your spreadsheet.

8. Center the data in your cells. To do this, click and drag over all of the data in your spreadsheet to highlight it. Then use the **Align Center** button on your toolbar (Figure 12-4).

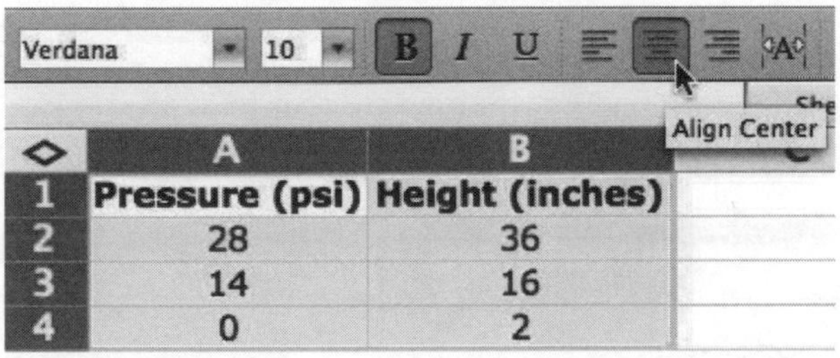

Figure 12-4

9. Now use your *Pressure* data to create a chart. First, highlight all of your data in both columns, including the labels. Choose the **Insert** menu, select **Chart**, and click on **Marked Line Chart** (Figure 12-5).

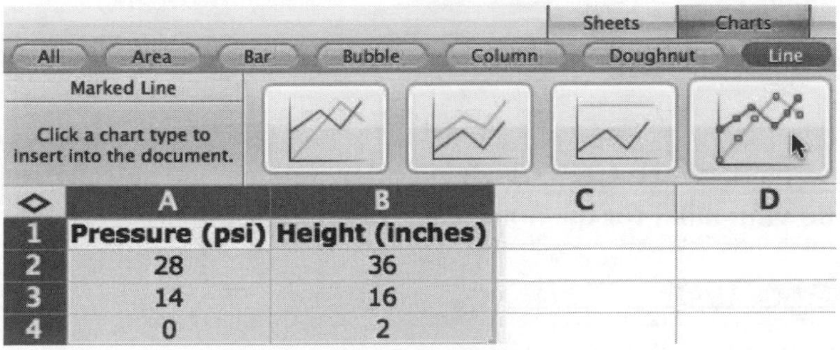

Figure 12-5

10. Your chart should now appear within your spreadsheet.

11. Go to the **Chart** menu, select **Move Chart**, choose **New Sheet,** and click **OK**.

12. Your chart should now take up the entire page.

Pressure Bounce! *(cont.)*

Technology Procedure *(cont.)*

13. Click on the blue line for "Pressure" and hit **Delete** on your keyboard. This will remove the pressure data from your spreadsheet (Figure 12-6).

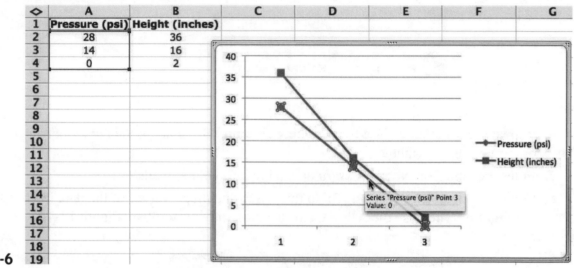

Figure 12-6

14. Next, under **Chart Options**, in the **Chart Title** box, type in: "Pressure vs. Height" (Figure 12-7).

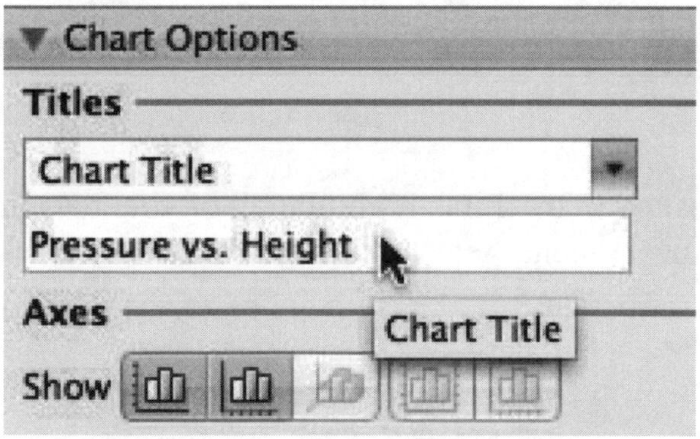

Figure 12-7

15. Under **Chart Options,** click on the **Chart Title** dropdown menu and select **Horizontal Category Axis**. Type in the following label for the horizontal axis: "Pressure" (Figure 12-8).

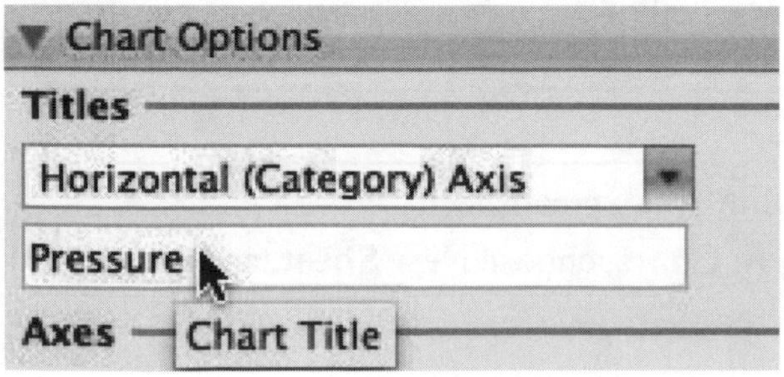

Figure 12-8

Pressure Bounce! *(cont.)*

Technology Procedure *(cont.)*

16. Next, go to the **Chart** menu and select **Source Data** to bring up the **Select Data Source** window.

17. Click on the small red arrow next to the **Category (x) Axis Labels** box (Figure 12-9).

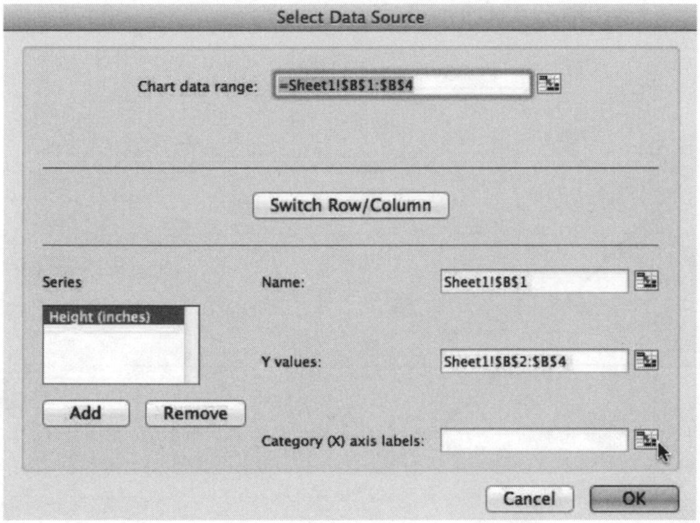

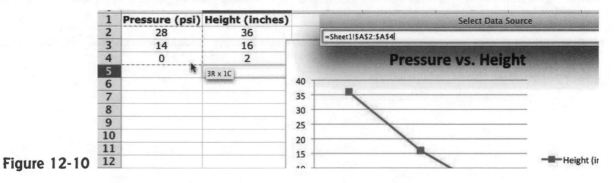

Figure 12-9

18. Now click and drag over only the numbers in column A of your spreadsheet, then hit the **Enter** key on your keyboard (Figure 12-10).

Figure 12-10

19. Hit the **Enter** key again and then click on **OK** in the **Select Data Source** window. This will put your *Pressure* data on your chart's horizontal axis (Figure 12-11).

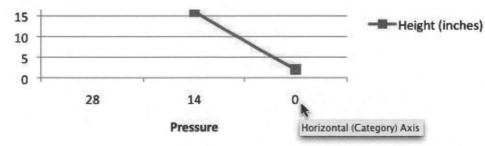

Figure 12-11

Pressure Bounce! *(cont.)*

Technology Procedure *(cont.)*

20. Your chart is now complete and should look similar to the one in Figure 12-12. **Save** and **Print.**

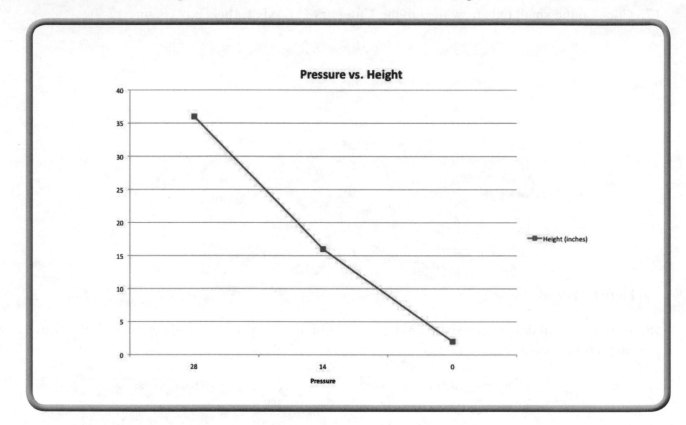

Figure 12-12